Palgrave CIBFR Studies in Islamic Finance

Series Editors
Nafis Alam
Henley Business School
University of Reading
Selangor, Malaysia

Syed Aun R. Rizvi
Suleman Dawood School of Business
Lahore University of Management Sciences
Lahore, Pakistan

The Centre for Islamic Business and Finance Research (CIBFR) is a global center of excellence for developing Islamic business and finance as a scientific academic discipline and for promoting Islamic financial products, monetary and fiscal policies, and business and trade practices. Based at The University of Nottingham campus in Malaysia, CIBFR looks at the multi-dimensional aspects of Islamic business, cutting across the major themes of Islamic economics, Islamic finance and the Halal market. True to the pioneering nature of the research CIBFR undertakes, the Palgrave CIBFR Series in Islamic Finance offers empirical enquiries into key issues and challenges in modern Islamic finance. It explores issues in such varied fields as Islamic accounting, Takaful (Islamic insurance), Islamic financial services marketing, and ethical and socially responsible investing.

More information about this series at
http://www.palgrave.com/gp/series/15190

Mohsin Ali · Najeeb Zada

The Islamic Finance Trading Framework

Legitimizing Profit Making

palgrave
macmillan

Mohsin Ali
Taylor's Business School
Taylor's University
Subang Jaya, Malaysia

Najeeb Zada
Department of Islamic Theology
Islamia College Peshawar
Peshawar, Pakistan

ISSN 2523-3483 ISSN 2523-3491 (electronic)
Palgrave CIBFR Studies in Islamic Finance
ISBN 978-3-319-96612-0 ISBN 978-3-319-96613-7 (eBook)
https://doi.org/10.1007/978-3-319-96613-7

This Palgrave Pivot imprint is published by the registered company Springer Nature Switzerland AG
The registered company address is: Gewerbestrasse 11, 6330 Cham, Switzerland

CONTENTS

List of Figures

CHAPTER 1

Introduction

Abstract This chapter tries to justify the reason of studying the impact of Islamisation on different academic and practical areas, specifically business and trade laws in Islam. This chapter briefly presents the history of the evolution of Islamic law (Sharia) in general and shows its significance in the modern world which gave birth to the subject of Islamic economics. We also summarise the most important aspects of Islamic business and trade law in this chapter which include Sharia compliant trading frameworks, trading under Islamic commercial law, trading practices and financial transactions prohibited under Islamic law, profit making in Islam and some other auxiliary issues.

Keywords Islamic law (Sharia) · Islamic economics · Aspects of Islamic business and trade law

With the rapid "Islamisation" in many areas of the world, an extensive research on Islamic law has considerably saturated the literature, though with multifaceted understandings and meanings projected by their authors, this topic still comprises ample research prospects. Entailing numerous branches, Islamic law also entails businesses and trade concept; the topic grabbed many economists', researchers', and practitioners' attention, likewise the topic under this book's discussion.

M. Ali and N. Zada, *The Islamic Finance Trading Framework*,
Palgrave CIBFR Studies in Islamic Finance,
https://doi.org/10.1007/978-3-319-96613-7_1

Islam a highly debated theology, influencing almost one-fifth of the world's population, prejudicially seen by multi-lensed perspectives, is usually misunderstood in today's world. It would be justifiable to explore any doctrine; one shall stretch back to the roots of that theology genuinely. Hence, rather than relying on the shallow image of Islam portrayed by world's media nowadays, the concept of Islamic economic system can be well grasped if be stretched back to its very roots, where Islamic economic setup was devised by Prophet Muhammad (peace be upon him) in his times by the command of Almighty Allah.

Islam, as not merely a set of commandments that guide its followers to achieve success in hereafter, is a holistic code of conduct which transforms the human life to achieve its pinnacle in all aspects: individual, social, economic, and political. Therefore, a society of Muslims, practicing Islamic rules in true essence and abiding their religious duties, can exhibit an ideal society of marvelous merits. Though a lot of conscientious efforts are being undertaken to achieve one, such a society of ideal setup can't be witnessed in today's world, except for centuries' old economy, flourished under the supervision of Prophet (peace be upon him) and his followers. This Islamic setup was not structured effortlessly. They had undergone agonizing circumstances before acquiring an Islamic state, where Islamic concepts were pragmatically and freely put into practice.

Its innate feature of human nature that it does not accept change in a sudden nature, rather a gradual and balanced influence, exhibits profound and lasting conduct. The foundations of the first Islamic economic setup, witnessed in the times of Prophet Muhammad (peace be upon him), were laid in parts. The pre-Islamic setup could not easily whip out abruptly. It takes years to inculcate the virtues of an Ideal system comprised of. The revelation of Quran, on which Islamic law is chiefly based, can be bifurcated into two parts: Makkan period, when Prophet Muhammad (peace be upon him) and his followers were in city of Makkah, and Madani period, the period when they migrated to city called "Yathrab" but named Madinah afterward because of the Prophet's stay in that city. Makkan period can be summarized as a tough and traumatized one, as Muslims had to face numerous challenges to survive with their new Muslim identity in a non-Muslim setup. However, Madani period can be categorized as one with affluence, free will, and harmony. Therefore, the Madani period demonstrated comparatively more reflective Islamic setup than Makkan, presumably the free will and liberty of

Muslims in the land. Holy revelations of Quran were therefore revealed by keeping very nature of human being into consideration. Earlier, during Makkan period, the prohibitions came out as disregarded or detested, but not in the form of strict prohibition, for example, wine and usury prohibitions. Later came the strict commandments requiring complete prohibitions of such matters. In this gradual transformational progression, all curses of usury, exploitation of power, ill means of wealth, oppressions of weak, and evils like riba came to an end, and an Islamic society was structured. With an extensive emphasis on justice, honesty, equality, empathy (system of zakat and usher), and welfare at large with interest-free economy, Islamic society laid the foundations of a role model to be worth idealized. This historic civilization demonstrated that Islam emphasizes not only on the physical and spiritual supplications for hereafter, but indeed motivates its followers to thrive in this world too. The prime reference of Islamic law, Quran the holy book, emphasizes the reconciliation between hereafter and worldly endeavors in the form of an important supplication which Muslims implore in their prayers, as: "Our Lord give us in this world which is good and in the hereafter that which is good, and save us from the torment of the fire" (Quran, 2:201). Therefore, following Islamic law connotes striking a balance between worldly life and hereafter. Henceforth, those who falsely claim this religion for inculcating monasticism should refer the very principal references before portraying such an image of Islam. Besides clear references from Quran and Hadith (sayings and acts of Prophet Muhammad peace be upon him), had not the fact enough for criticizers that how Muslim scholars excelled in endeavoring marvelous accomplishments in the field of science and arts, which civilizations followed for? Certainly, an imperative need arises to undertake a fair and thorough analysis in order to surface a just opinion.

Since Islamic law necessitates adherence to both divine and worldly perspectives, this holistic legal system also shapes one's dealings in means of earnings and occupations. For the reason that choosing business as one's occupation is highly esteemed in Islamic economic setup, Muslim world encompasses a large majority of business owners, whose individual lives are being shaped by Islamic law, so as their business dealings. One cannot isolate religious duties to worldly ones if following Islamic law. As mentioned in Quran, "Surely my prayer and my sacrifice and my life and my death are (all) for Allah, the Lord of the worlds" (Quran: 6162). Therefore, striving for worldly affluence is not at all condemned in

Islam, but certainly not beyond the boundaries of religious prohibitions. Islamic economic system can well be explained as a system of production, resource allocation, and distribution of goods and services within a society, where all these practices are administered under Shariah law (sacred law of Islam). When a whole social order is being directed under such teachings, an Islamic economic setup forms, necessitating equity, justice, economic freedom, honesty, and uprightness observed meticulously. According to Muslim thinkers, the concept of welfare which economic system brings into the economy has to be confined within Islamic framework. Hence, in Islamic economic system, there is no concept of welfare if there is any defiance from Shariah.

Many Islamic economists, thinkers, researchers, and practitioners are seeking ways to pragmatically align the Islamic economic principles and practical frameworks. There is not a single work of knowledge, whose thinkers don't have differences of opinion and thought that is healthy to bring diversification and innovation, but lack of one positive course of conduct is earnestly needed for practical enforcement of Islamic economic system. The thorough and diligent work of Islamic economists is commendable in pursuing Islamic economic system; still, for achieving economic development goals of Islamic world, a lot of issues are under evolutionary phase to come up with unanimously agreed solutions. Consequently, avenue of Islamic economic system still demands a solemn and thorough research to pave the way for solutions of such issues. Discussing such compelling issues of the Islamic commercial law can lay the very foundations of Islamic economic development.

This book is designed for both Islamic and conventional finance practitioners, policy-makers, and students of Islamic law, economics and finance. It can serve as a guide to be well acquainted with compelling issues of Islamic commercial law.

With extensive emphasis on equity, justice, economic freedom, and welfare, Islamic commercial law puts consumer protection a great precedence over financial innovation, as it can lead to "Gharar," which is prohibited in Islamic commercial law. Islamic commercial law, though does not abrogate financial solidification, rather it regulates and outcast those practices which can jeopardize economic development, like financial transactions involving "Riba" (riba and gharar explained later in the book's chapter). By means of financial innovation, many speculative instruments used in today's conventional financial transactions, at times, render the economic system into a complete failure, as witnessed in economic crisis 2007–2008. Beginning part of this book is primarily reserved for elaboration of such prohibited contracts, transactions and practices in Islamic commercial law, and important insights regarding the issues.

All the religions and doctrines followed in this world have faced once or many sheer criticism and opposition from masses; however, the hatred and prejudice Islam has encountered are incomparable. With incomprehensible abhorrence and conspiracies against it, its true picture has been blurred through misinterpretation of its beliefs and rubrics. The religion which abstains its followers from killing civilians, public, and even trees in the most fervent circumstances of war is labeled as religion associated with terrorism. By the same token, a religion which places utter emphasis on balancing spirituality with worldly matters is deemed to be ultraconservative and stale enough that it curbs its followers from undertaking financial transaction in this modern competitive world. This is truly a discriminating treatment of this doctrine, when seen from a prejudiced lens, and hence needed a fair and deep analysis before crafting any label on it. Islam is not merely a set of beliefs for personal connection with God confined just to houses of worship, rather a code of life from womb to tomb that cannot be isolated from any matter related to life, be it business, economics, law, politics, or any aspect. Henceforth, as soon as many Asian and African Islamic countries have politically liberated from Western rules, the need for tailoring the country-wide system to their very own beliefs and philosophies became more and more eminent among their scholars and practitioners. The globalization, technological advancement along with independence of Muslim countries paved the way for including Shariah into amount of commercial and civil laws. Therefore, a part of the book has also addressed the issue of businesses and trade activities under Islamic commercial law.

Another compelling issue, discussed in this book, is where Islamic finance industry stands in today's competitive financial innovation and financial deepening arena. Rapid globalization has instigated the researchers and practitioners from Islamic world to devise economic system, conforming to Islamic law, which can substitute the conventional interest-based economic scheme. Consequently, they have come up with, though not just confined to, prohibitions of "riba" and "Gharar," but also the development of Islamic financial instruments. There is a bunch of such contracts that are utilized to fulfill the needs of the customers in the Islamic finance industry, yet still are under development stage, challenging their conventional counterparts in financial markets.

These contracts, due to the complex nature of the products offered by financial institutions, are used in a group to structure particular product, using financial engineering techniques and methods. Since Islamic financial contracts are derived from Shariah, that need to be combined and observe certain parameters which indeed is a challenging task. Accounting and Auditing Organization for Islamic Financial Institutions (AAOFI) is aiding in this matter by providing detailed guidelines for the combination of contracts. Though still under evolutionary process, Islamic financial products are challenging their counterparts by fulfilling their customer financial needs in a Shariah compliant manner.

We have also included discussion on the differences and similarities between Islamic and conventional trading frameworks. Islamic framework is found to be quite compatible with conventional trading framework barring some exceptions which are both practical and philosophical. We have discussed how Islamic trading framework provides more comprehensive and effective way of dealings. We have also discussed the impacts of these trading frameworks on the economies at large. Bringing this discussion forward, we have allocated a whole chapter on the discussion on profit, where we elaborate on how Islam promotes earning profit through fair means but at the same time the philosophy of profit-making in Islam is quite different from the conventional mind-set.

Some auxiliary issues in Islamic trading framework are also heightened in this book. Individual rights are strongly protected in Islamic economic system, presumably the strong ethical base it is erected on. Artificial pampering of markets through tariffs, quotas, and the like is not regarded in Islamic economic system, but indeed some dire issues solemnly require government intervention into the markets. Income disproportionality, poverty elevations, unsatisfied public needs, and environmental degradation are those issues which cannot be left unattended; therefore, government has to play its role in alleviating these issues. Though economic system structured on Islamic principles embodies equity, honesty, justice, and ethical system for common welfare, still a more channelized and dedicated effort is needed in emerging idea of corporate social responsibility (CSR).

CHAPTER 2

Trading Under Islamic Commercial Law

Abstract This chapter provides a comprehensive introduction to the concept and application of trading under Islamic commercial law. As a religion, Islam does not distinguish between wordly and spiritual affairs of life. Instead, both these are intertwined in a balanced manner. An act like trade and business which may appear a mundane life activity is regarded spiritual by Islam if conducted as per the rules and conditions laid by Islamic commercial law. Accordingly, this law provides a comprehensive list of activities, practices and transactions which are deemed impermissible and prohibited. Similarly, it provides a list of different types of contracts that can be undertaken to fulfil the basic needs of human society. Accordingly, this chapter digs deep into these two and further explores the mechanism of consumer protection that is embedded inside the prohibited and permissible elements of Islamic commercial law. In terms of Islamic law and jurisprudence, such protection comes in the form of different types of options available to consumers which ensure that their rights and property are protected completely, but not at the stake of businessmen and dealers simultaneously.

Keywords Islamic law · Riba · Gharar · Maysir · Option

M. Ali and N. Zada, *The Islamic Finance Trading Framework*,
Palgrave CIBFR Studies in Islamic Finance,
https://doi.org/10.1007/978-3-319-96613-7_2

Introduction

Islamic law, also referred to as Shariah, governs the whole life of an individual, from the time before one is born until and even after death. It emphasizes on proper conduct in all matters including one's intention and areas pertaining to worship, transactions, and judgments. State and religion are not separated and even worldly acts by an individual are considered as worship if done with good faith and performed in a way prescribed by Islamic law. It does not treat ethics and morality outside the boundary of the mundane affairs of human life. The entire human life is composed of serving the Creator if the tenants of Shariah are properly observed. Trade and commerce are no exception to this general rule and this is what distinguishes Islam from other man-made systems where a clear demarcation exists between worldly and religious affairs. In fact, Shariah declares a very high status for an honest tradesman. The Prophet Muhammad (SAW) himself was a trader before prophethood was assigned to him. Consequently, the Muslim jurists have developed a detailed theory of trade and business which one finds to be revived today in the Islamic financial system which is grooming fast around the globe. The principles laid down by Muslim jurists to construct Islamic commercial law is the foundation of contemporary Islamic finance which has flourished during the past few decades and has attracted the attention of many, especially in the wake of the global financial crisis.

The term "commercial law" is not used in a unanimous meaning even under existing man-made legal systems. Thus, this term denotes only transactions but not institutions under the common law. However, its equivalents in civil law encompass both transactions and institutions. In addition, there is further disagreement even among the Western systems with respect to the use of the term commercial law. Some systems make a formal distinction between commercial and non-commercial law but others do not. For instance, no such distinction exists in Italy. Even the USA does not make a formal distinction between commercial and non-commercial law in contracts which is in contrast to what is found under the French law. However, the first dichotomy between institutions and transactions does not apply in the case of Shariah mainly due to the nonexistence of legal personality, even though there are contracts that resemble current-day partnerships. With respect to the distinction between commercial and non-commercial law, although categorization of Shariah was made by jurists, it broadly consisted of akhlaq (morals), ʿibadah (religious observance), and muʿamalat (transactions). Besides, the jurists also recognized the difference between commercial and non-commercial contracts but it was not similar to the one found in West today (Foster, 2006).

There is an additional factor that puts Shariah in contrast to these systems. In Shariah, the same principles of morality apply to all situations and all spheres of life. Thus, a believer is expected to behave in the same manner whether at home or at office. This is not the case with Western systems which ask for different attitudes and moral standards for commercial and non-commercial transactions. To sum up, Shariah shares some features with other legal systems of the world but it also has some unique characteristics of it.

Contract Under Islamic Law: Definition and Types

The Arabic word for contract is *aqd* which literally means tying up or to knot. This word is also found in Quran which is the main source of Shariah. The concept of *aqd* is very broad in Shariah as it is applied to contracts and obligations of many types. It encompasses an individual's obligations toward God, the political obligations contained in treaties, the interpersonal obligations of marriage, and the commercial obligations of the contracting parties involved in different types of contracts. The underlying principle of all these obligations is the Quranic injunction that contracts must be fulfilled. In its general sense, the term contract can be defined as a two-party transaction which consists of an offer from one side and an acceptance from the other (Hassan, 2002). According to the famous *Majallat al-Ahkam al-Adliyyah* which is a codified form of Islamic civil law, a contract is defined as the connection of an offer with an acceptance in a lawful manner which marks its effect on the subject of that connection (The Mejelle, Article 103). However, there might be contracts from one side too—a guarantee, gift, or bequeath. There is disagreement among the modern scholars as to whether a general theory of contracts, i.e., general default rules, applies to all contracts. Arguments exist on both sides (Hassan, 2002). However, it is difficult to deny that Islamic law of contract is comprehensive as well as flexible by nature and its application in the form of modern Islamic finance contracts is an evidence of this claim.

A term related to aqd is wa'ad (promise) which has got significant importance in the context of contemporary Islamic finance. Traditionally, a promise made by one party is not legally binding as per Islamic law, although it is the moral responsibility of the promising party to fulfill its promise and breaking of promise is strongly despised in Shariah. In modern Islamic finance, promise has been declared as legally binding on the basis of the ruling in the Maliki School. This stance has been taken in order to make customers fulfill their promises (to purchase a commodity from an Islamic bank) toward Islamic banks in order to save the later from losses which may result from non-fulfillment of promise by the customer. Nevertheless, such promise is not synonymous to a formal contract under Islamic law and differences do exist between a legally binding promise and a formal/valid contract.

Generally speaking, the commercial contracts in Islamic law are broadly categorized into exchange-based contracts and charity-based contracts. In exchange-based contracts, the transacting parties enter into a contract to acquire ownership of an asset or commodity for a price. The contracts in this category end up in the transfer of ownership. On the other hand, the parties in a charity-based contract do not have such intention; instead, they are based on benevolence and cooperation (ISRA, 2011). It is the first category of contracts that will be the main focus in our case.

In terms of the legal status, i.e., whether a contract is valid or otherwise, a contract is divided into three types: valid, voidable, and void. If all conditions and accessories required for validity are met in a contract, it is valid. However, a voidable contract is the one which contains the essential elements of a valid contract but lacks some additional/nonessential attributes. This logically leads us to the definition of a void contract in which some essential pillar of a valid contract is missing (Ayub, 2009).

A sale contract can also be divided on the basis of the time of price payment and delivery of subject matter. As a general rule, both price and subject matter need to be exchanged immediately following the conclusion of contract. However, it may be the case that one of these is deferred to some specific time in future. If the payment of both counter values is mandatory at the time of contract, it is called sarf (currency exchange contract). If price is paid on the spot but the subject matter is to be delivered in the future, it is known as salam contract. In the reverse case, i.e., the subject matter is delivered on spot but the price is to be laid in future (either in full or in installments), the contract is known as bay muajjal or deferred payment sale. It is noteworthy that the deferment of both price and subject matter, commonly known as bay al-kali bi al-kali is not allowed under Islamic law (Saleem, 2013).

Yet another classification is based on the determination and nature of price. If the contracting parties agree upon the price of, for instance, a piece of land without bothering about and any reference to the cost price, it is known as a bargain (musawamah) sale. However, if the seller discloses the price to the buyer, then the sale can be concluded in three possible ways. The seller either concludes a deal with buyer at exactly the cost price without earning any profit, or earns some profit over and above the cost price, or incurs some loss by selling the item at lower than cost price. These types are known as tawliyah (sale with no profit), murabahah (sale with cost plus profit), and wadi'ah (sale with loss), respectively. It is pertinent to note that in contemporary Islamic finance, it is cost-plus-profit mode of sale which is predominantly adopted by and practiced in Islamic financial institutions (Saleem, 2013).

Another classification of sale contract is based on the nature of two compensations exchanged. If the compensations are non-fungible, like the exchange of a dress with an animal, it is known as exchange sale. However, if a non-fungible is exchanged for a fungible item, it is known as a general sale which is the most common type of sale. If both the compensations are currency, the sale is known as sarf (currency exchange), whereas the exchange of a liability as the object of sale for a non-fungible price is known as salam (Al-Zuhayli, 2007).

Contracts Under Islamic Commercial Law: Pillars and Ethics

According to the majority of Muslim jurists, there are four essential pillars of a sale contract: the contracting parties (seller and buyer), the object of sale, the price, and expression/wording/language of the contract. The wording of sale contract consists of an offer and an acceptance. An offer is the expression made by the first party to the contract, be it buyer or seller. Acceptance is what follows an offer. Both offer and acceptance should be in accordance with each other. Traditionally, offer and acceptance should take place in the same session in order to comply with the stipulation of unity of session. However, the contemporary scholars allow online and other forms of sale where the parties are not present in the same session provided that certain conditions are met and all types of uncertainties are removed by agreeing on detailed terms and conditions. In any case, Bakar (2003) maintains that Islamic law is distinct from other legal systems in that it insists on the session of contract, whereby both offer and acceptance are to be jointly connected in a single session without any gap in time or place.

The Muslim jurists also allow a particular type of sale which takes place without any express language or offer and acceptance. This is known as sale by conduct. For instance, a buyer and seller may agree on the exchange of an object against a price without expressing their agreement, and even offer and acceptance, in words. But they both know and are agreed over the price and the object of sale. This form of sale has become a norm nowadays where automated process relieves one from time-consuming processes of contract including any physical contact with the other (seller/buyer) party.

For a sale contract to be valid under Islamic law, there are general conditions that must be present in all types of sale contracts. These essentials are related to the four pillars of a contract referred to above. Regarding the parties to the contract, they must be legally competent to enter into contract. There are two aspects regarding measurement of the competence of contracting parties in Islamic law: prudence and puberty (Bakar, 2003). Thus, an insane person or a minor does not have the legal capacity to enter into a contract.

With respect to the expression of a contract, Islamic law allows it to be oral or written. As mentioned earlier, even sale by conduct with no verbal and written offer and acceptance is deemed permissible. In addition, it is also required that offer and acceptance should take place in the same session. According to Bakar (2003), the stipulation that offer and acceptance should take place in the same session is a unique feature of Islamic law which distinguishes it from other legal systems of the world. Offer and acceptance must also be such that price, place, and date of delivery are precisely determined and fixed.

For a sale to be valid, the **subject matter** of the contract should be permissible under Shariah and should also be alienable. Likewise, the owner of the subject matter should take the related ownership risks in order to be eligible for profit. The subject matter must also exist at the time of sale and a nonexistent item cannot be sold. It is also required that the object of sale is precisely determined and that the seller has it in his ownership. Apart from ownership, the seller also needs to have it in his possession. But the possession need not be physical as it can also be constructive (Ayub, 2009).

Apart from the legal requirements mentioned above, there are certain commands related to the code of ethics and moral that Islamic law prescribes in trade and commerce. Hassan (2007) divides this moral code into practices encouraged and those which are discouraged or prohibited in Shariah. The first category includes: being mindful of doubtful property and work, starting business from early morning, trustfulness in business transactions, generosity in bargaining and modesty in claiming debts, giving time to distressed debtor to pay his debts, generosity in business, and voluntary recession of an unwanted sale contract. On the other hand, business transactions in mosque, raising voices in the market, false swearing, lying or hiding facts in a sale, and fraudulent activities in trade are discouraged and prohibited. Similarly, Zuhayli (2007) maintains that ethical considerations in sale contract include: the avoidance of excessive profits, truthful and complete disclosure of information, ease of conduct, avoidance of swearing (even if truthful), frequent paying of charity, and documentation and witnessing of all debts.

Elements Prohibited in Islamic Commercial Contracts

Apart from the moral and ethical injunctions regarding the prohibition of certain practices, Islamic law has explicitly prohibited some practices. These prohibitions are at the core of Islamic commercial law and these include, inter alia, the prohibition of riba (interest), gharar (grave uncertainty), and maysir (gambling).

Riba is an Arabic word which literally means increase and includes all gains from loans and debts and anything over and above the principal of loans and debts and covers all forms of "interest" on commercial or personal loans (Ayub, 2009, p. 47). Therefore, the payment and receipt of interest as practices by conventional banks are prohibited under Islamic law. However, it is noteworthy that the term riba is far broader in its application and meaning. It includes other elements and practices too. Accordingly, the Muslim jurists, inferring from the different sources of Shariah, divide riba into two broad categories: riba in loan/debt transactions and riba in exchange transactions. An example of the first is bank interest which is prohibited. An example of the second category may include the sale of one kilogram of good quality wheat for two kilograms of cheap quality wheat. Riba in exchange is primarily prohibited in Hadith literature just as the first type is explicitly prohibited in Quran. It is worth mentioning that riba is condemned with the strongest possible expression in Quran; it has been declared against Allah and

His Messenger. Additionally, riba is also prohibited in other Abrahamic religions.

Scholars have presented different views as to why riba is prohibited? According to Saleem (2013), interest, whether the loan is taken for investment or consumption, causes injustice. This is because there are four possible situations once money is borrowed. The borrower may make sufficient profit to repay the capital plus interest and keep the balance; he may only earn profit to pay back the interest and capital without any balance left for him; there may not be any profit at all and only return the capital and interest by any means; and losses may be incurred by the borrower. This interest-based transaction is not fair even in the first case where the borrower has earned sufficient profit to pay back the lender and keep a share from profit because the borrower in this case may have returned a very small percentage to lender and kept a large share of profit for himself (or the case may be vice versa). Consequently, interest charged on productive/investment loan can also be exploitative to either or both the parties.

Regardless of what the possible cause for such prohibition is, a consensus has been reached among the contemporary Muslim scholars that riba in all its forms, especially in the form of bank interest, is prohibited (Hasan, 2014).

The second fundamental prohibition under Islamic commercial law is related to **gharar** which literally means hazard, risk, or grave uncertainty. In simple words, it refers to excessive uncertainty caused by lack of clarity regarding the subject matter or the price in a contract of exchange (Ayub, 2009). In its technical sense, gharar includes selling something which is not present at the time of sale, or the sale of something, the outcome of which is not known. Likewise, gharar may also include selling something about which it is not certain whether it will come into existence later on. Examples may include the selling of fish which is still in the water, or the selling of fetus in the womb of animal. The reason for the prohibition of gharar includes the possibility of fraud because the seller may obtain price from buyer but may not be able to deliver the sold item later on. Additionally, the scenarios of gharar possibly lead to disputes and disagreements between the parties which Islamic law wants to block by any means (Bakar, 2003).

The prohibition of gharar is based on the rule of justice and fair dealings because the existence of gharar in a transaction may lead to injustice and loss of properties to one or both the parties to the contract. If the outcome of a contract is unknown to the parties, it will expose them to unnecessary risk which will lead to subsequent disputes between them. Ultimately, it can be said that gharar is a means of blocking future disputes between the contracting parties (ISRA, 2016).

According to Zuhayli (2007), gharar is purposive cheating and deception as well as ignorance of the object of sale and un-deliverability of the object. Gharar may occur in a variety of ways including through un-deliverability of the object of sale, the nonexistence or ignorance of the object of sale, lack of full ownership of the object by the seller, or in any of a number of other forms.

However, it is noteworthy that the law itself accommodates gharar in certain contracts, like salam and istisna, once reasonable measures are taken to restrict the gharar factor within tolerable limits. Similarly, in gratuity contracts like gift, bequeath, and will, gharar is tolerated. It is also noteworthy that the prohibition of gharar is unique to Islamic law unlike the prohibition of riba which is propagated by other religions too. Additionally, many modern financial contracts and instruments like swaps and some types of derivative instruments are opposed by scholars due to the element of gharar in them.

Maysir which means gambling is the third explicit prohibition in Islamic commercial law. The word literally means ease. Since the money earned through gambling is made with ease, the relationship between literal and technical meaning is evident. According to Quran, gambling does contain some benefits for the people. However, the evils and miseries it causes them are far greater when compared with such benefits. Maysir is found in many financial instruments today which make them impermissible from Shariah perspective. For instance, conventional insurance is prohibited due to the existence of maysir. Similar is the case with prize bonds as well as some other types of lotteries and lucky draws.

Consumer Protection Under Islamic Commercial Law: The Concept of Khiyar (Option)

Once a sale contract has been concluded with all its essentials fulfilled, it becomes binding upon the parties. Its effect in the form of transfer of ownership is established and the parties are bound to fulfill their contractual obligations. However, Islamic law is cognizant of the exceptional circumstances, whereby a contract will need to be reviewed and canceled due to certain reasons. Such reasons can be many. For instance, one of the parties may need further time to consult experts regarding the contract. It may similarly be the case that a party wants to make sure that the subject matter is according to his expectations as well as the description of seller and is not defected. These and other reasons are recognized by Islamic law on the grounds that no party should face unwanted and unnecessary consequences as a result of the sale transaction. Toward this end, the Muslim jurists have elaborated the theory of khiyar or option which addresses these and other similar situations, whereby one of the parties has the right to rescind the contract even after its conclusion.

The notion of khiyar or option is somewhat unique to Islamic law. In common law, for instance, it is the responsibility of the buyer to be cautious when entering into a transaction, a rule generally known as *caveat emptor*. However, Islamic law tends to give more protection to buyer which may be due to the fact that the seller is more aware of the potential issues/defects of the subject matter, whereas the buyer is ignorant of such issues. The norm in Islamic law, therefore, is that the seller should be aware and should not try to deceive the buyer intentionally or unintentionally. Therefore, both the parties are protected from harm by providing them with different types of options respectively. However, option in this context is different from options in conventional financial terms which is a financial instrument in the derivative market, whereas the one in our case is a legal term related to post-contract scenarios under Islamic law.

Although there are as many as 17 types of options discussed by Muslim jurists, the most important options are briefly explained below.

Option of Session

As discussed earlier, both offer and acceptance should be in the same session. However, once an offer has been made by one of the parties, this party has the right to retreat from its offer as long as it is not accepted by the other party. If he retreats in time, his offer will cease to exist and any acceptance by the other party will have no legal effect. But once an acceptance is issued by the other party, then the party making an offer does not have the option to retreat from his offer.

Option of Defect

Under Islamic law, it is the responsibility of the seller to disclose all the defects in the subject matter of sale. In case something is sold with a defect and the buyer is unaware of this defect, he has the right to either cancel the sale or accept it with the price he had paid. Just like the existence of a defect gives rise to this option, it is also established in case that a specific feature is missing in the object of sale. In both cases, the buyer has the right to accept the contract or to cancel it.

Option of Stipulation

In some situations, any of the two contracting parties may need some time to ponder over the sale contract after the sale conclusion. In such a situation, Islamic law gives option to both the parties to stipulate at the time of contract that he will have the option to cancel the contract within a specific period of time (usually three days). This option enables both parties to consult experts about the item and decide accordingly. But limiting it to three days restricts them to utilize the option within reasonable time to allow the other party to dispose it off within a proper time frame.

Option of Inspection

At times, an item may be sold without being inspected by the buyer. In this case, the buyer has the right to investigate the item after he sees it and to find out if all the features described at the time of sale contract are present in the item. In case the buyer feels that the deal is not in his favor, he has the right to cancel the contract after inspecting the item.

Option of Price Payment

This option is found in cases when something is sold on credit basis. The seller may stipulate at the time of concluding a credit sale that in case the buyer does not pay the price within three days, the deal will be canceled. This option protects the seller from unwanted delay in price payment by the buyer.

Fraud Option

In this case, the buyer is deceived with respect to amount of price or quality of the sale item. For instance, the seller may put the best quality items on top of a display but underlying it is the worst quality. Similarly, the seller may claim that the price is as per the market custom but it may be very high than the customary market rate in which case the buyer has the right to cancel the contract.

Prohibited Trading Practices and Transactions Under Islamic Law

There are specific types of transactions and sale contracts that are prohibited under Islamic commercial law. All these types were prevalent in the Arab society before the advent of Islam. However, their very nature was exploitative and contained harm to one or both the parties. Therefore, they were prohibited mainly because they consisted of some prohibited elements like gharar. On the other hand, as we shall discuss in the next chapter, those contracts that did not contain any prohibitive element and were not harmful to any party were retained by Islamic law.

Some well-known prohibited contracts and trading practices include the following.

Sale by Throwing Stone

As its name suggests, this type of sale was conducted by throwing stones. Accordingly, the vendor and purchaser would agree that a stone would be thrown in the air and whichever cloth, camel, or sheep it fell upon would have to be bought by the purchaser. This transaction was prohibited because it contained the element of gharar.

Sale by Touching

This was a sale contract in which a piece of folded cloth would be bought or sold merely by touching. The buyer was not allowed to open and inspect the cloth and even both the parties would renounce their right of option in advance. This sale was prohibited by Islamic law.

Sale by Throwing

Under this practice, a piece of cloth or an article would be thrown from one contracting party to the other to signify the sale. Both parties would throw, for instance, a garment to each other without inspecting it and each garment would be considered a compensation for the other.

Sale by Description

Under this transaction, an item would be sold without possession or inspection. It would only be described while the delivery was to be made at some later stage.

Sale of Unspecified for Specified

In this sale, fruit of a known weight would be sold for fruits in bulk which were unspecified in weight, measure, or number. For instance, a definite measure of ripe dates would be sold for an unknown amount of green dates.

Sale of Fruits Before Ripening Appears

Here, fruits and vegetables or grains would be sold by the owners before they started to ripen. The very nature of the transaction was such that it would result in a lot of disputes because of the unknown loses that would occur at the later stage. Therefore, this practice was prohibited by Islam.

Sale of Fetus

This refers to the sale of fetus of an animal. It also included the sale of an animal which would be brought forth later from the fetus itself. Thus, the parties would imply that a she-camel would give birth first and then offspring would later become pregnant after growing up. Again this sale was declared void by Islam (Saleem, 2013).

Sale of Haram (Prohibited) Items

Certain items are declared prohibited by Islam and these cannot be bought or sold. Examples include blood, wine, pork, dead animal, and the like.

Sale of Nonexistent Objects

If the object of sale does not exist at the time of sale, though it is permissible per se, it cannot be sold—for instance, the sale of fetus or the sale of fruits and plants before they appear. Other examples of the sale of non-existent include the sale of the male camel's sperms, the sale of female camel's eggs, the sale of pearls in the shell, milk in an udder, and wool on the back of sheep; these sales are prohibited because of the ignorance or uncertainty about the quality and volume of the object of sale.

Sale of Undeliverable Objects

An originally permissible subject matter of sale which cannot be delivered also falls under the prohibition. Examples include a bird that flew away from its owner, runaway camels, wild cows, and the like (Zuhayli, 2007).

Sale of Meat for Animal

It is also not permissible to sell a living animal for slaughtered meat.

Combination of Sale and Loan

Sale and loan cannot be combined in such a way that they form part of the same dealing. For instance, A sells his car to B and as a result of this bargain B will lend him a specific amount of money.

Deferment of Both Price and Subject Matter

If a sale contract is concluded with permissible object but neither the price is paid on spot nor the subject matter is delivered, it is also not permissible (Bakar, 2003).

Fraudulent Overbidding

If two parties are in the middle of concluding a deal and they are busy in bargaining, it is not permissible for a third party which has no intention to buy the item to induce the buyer to offer a higher price. The third party here has no intention to buy the item; he only wants the potential buyer to increase the price offered and this situation is usually pre-planned between the third party and the seller. This is contrast to bidding which is allowed in Islam.

Concealment of Defects

Cheating and concealment of defects were a common practice in pre-Islamic Arabia but this practice was denounced by Islam (Saleem, 2013). If a buyer is deceived by such means, Islam gives him the right to opt for the sale or to exit from it once the real situation is known to him. This is contrast to the common law system where the buyer should be careful and he needs to save himself from such situation.

Meeting Caravan Outside the City

In case there is a caravan approaching the city, it is not permissible for someone to go outside the city and buy the stuff from caravan (Zuhayli, 2007), especially when those in caravan do not know the price that could be offered to them in the city or when the people in the city are in need of the items brought by the caravan.

Thus, one can see that the prohibition of these different kinds of practices and sales aims to serve justice among the individuals and the society at large. This also shows the proactive nature of Islamic commercial law in particular, whereby the means to exploitation and injustice are blocked by declaring such practices prohibited and void.

Prohibited Types of Sale Due to Gharar

Gharar is more related to "uncertainty" than to risk. This uncertainty is generally linked to the presence of the subject matter, rights of the parties, and the outcomes of the contract. Gharar as discussed earlier may also be defined as trickery through unawareness by parties to a contract. Following are some types of sales which have been prohibited by Prophet (SAW) due to gharar:

Prohibited types of sale due to Gharar

1	Bai'	Al-Ma'doum	Nonexistent
2	Bai'	Al-Khattar	Items in danger of not being found
3	Bai'	Al-Mahameen	Sperm of male animals
4	Bai'	Al-Maliqih	Eggs of female animals
5	Bai'	Al-Nabal al-Habala	Fetus in womb of female animals
6	Bai'	Al-Ma'jouz	Something impossible to deliver
7	Bai'	Al-Qanis	something before possessing it
8	Bai'	Al-Gha'iss	Divers catch before seeing it

9	Bai'	Al-Muzabana	Fruit on tree for dates/money
10	Bai'	Al-Muhaqala	Harvested wheat for unharvested
11	Bai'	Al-Mulmasa	By touch
12	Bai'	Al-Munabaza	By throwing
13	Bai'	Al-Hassat	By stone
14	Bai'	Al-Majhoul	Of unknown
15	Bai'	Al-Jahal bi al-Ajal	If unknown time for credit
16	Bai'	Al-Jahl bi al-Mabi'	Unknown quantity/size/weight, etc.
17	Bai'	Al-Jahl bi al-Thaman	If price/cost unknown
18	Bai'	Al-Jahl bi Jinsithaman aw Mathnoun	When kind/quantity of goods is elsewhere
19	Bai'	Atan fi Bai	Is two sales in one deal + one conditional upon other
20	Bai'	Ma la Yurja Salamatauh	Near death animal/slave
21	Bai'	Al-Mutamal-Wujudh	What may not be present
22	Bai'	Al-Muhtamal-Taslimuh	What may not be delivered
23	Bai'	Wa shart	If with a condition
24	Bai'	Al-Ghaib	The invisible
25	Bai'	Al-Thamara	Seeds of tree before they become fruit
26	Bai'	Majhoul bi Majhoul	Unknown for unknown
27	Bai'	Al-Souf	Wool still on sheep
28	Bai'	Al-Laban fi Dhari'	Milk in udders of cow
29	Bai'	Bidoun haq al-Tasaruf	Without right to possession
30	Bai'	Al-Hayat Wa-maout	For limit of life or after death
31	Bai'	Al-Dayn	Sale of debt
32	Bai'	Al-Arbun	Downpayment sale

Source http://www.islamicthinkers.com/index/index.php?option=com_content&task=view&id=195&Itemid=26

Conclusion

Whether Islamic commercial law could give a comprehensive theory of contract or not is still debated among the scholars. However, it is evident from the discussion in this chapter that Islamic commercial law has provided a comprehensive list of contracts that are permissible and those which are prohibited. Islam as a religion did not abrogate the earlier practices, especially in the sphere of commerce and finance, outrightly. Instead, it canceled only those contracts which were based on exploitation and injustice. On the other hand, it retained some contracts in their entirety, as we shall see in the coming chapter, while modifications were introduced in a number of other contracts. We also observed in this chapter that Islam has strictly prohibited riba in all its forms. However, Islamic law is unique in the sense that it also put a complete ban on gharar and this feature is not found in other religions. No wonder why Islamic finance was spared from the miseries of the global financial crisis in 2007–2008. Many practices and instrument especially those in the derivatives market could not find acceptance from Shariah scholars. Consequently, Islamic financial institutions are by and large safe from such practices so far, with the exception of a few practices in some jurisdictions. Likewise, we also observed that consumer protection has a special space in Islamic commercial law and this is evident from the theory of options or khiyarat as discussed in this chapter.

The next chapter will further elaborate on the nature, modes, and types of contracts which are permissible under Islamic commercial law. The chapter will also elucidate on some contested contracts found in contemporary Islamic finance sphere.

References

Al-Zuhayli, W. (2007). *Financial transactions in Islamic jurisprudence* (M. A. el-Gamal, Trans.). Beirut: Dar al-fikir al-Mauaser.

Ayub, M. (2009). *Understanding Islamic finance*. Chichester: Wiley.

Bakar, M. D. (2003). Contracts in Islamic commercial and their application in modern Islamic financial system. *Iqtisad Journal of Islamic Economics,* 30–44.

Foster, N. H. (2006). Encounters between legal systems: Recent cases concerning Islamic commercial law in secular courts. *Amicus Curiae, 68,* 2–9.

Hasan, Z. (2014). *Islamic banking and finance: An integrative approach*. Oxford: Oxford University Press.

Hassan, A. A. H. (2007). *Sales and contracts in early Islamic commercial law*. Petaling Jaya: The Other Press.

Hassan, H. (2002). Contracts in Islamic law: The principles of commutative justice and liberality. *Journal of Islamic Studies, 13*(3), 257–297.

ISRA. (2011). *Islamic financial system: Principles and operations*. Kuala Lumpur, Malaysia: International Shari'ah Research Academy for Islamic Finance (ISRA).

ISRA. (2016). *Islamic financial system: Principles and operations* (2nd ed.). Kuala Lumpur, Malaysia: International Shari'ah Research Academy for Islamic Finance (ISRA).

Saleem, M. Y. (2013). *Islamic commercial law*. Singapore: Wiley.

The Mejelle. (n.d.). *Being an English translation of Majallah al-Ahkam al-'Adliyyah and a complete code on Islamic civil law* (C. R. Tyser, Trans.). Lahore: Law Publishing. http://www.islamicthinkers.com/index/index.php?option=com_content&task=view&id=195&Itemid=26.

CHAPTER 3

Application of Islamic Financial Contracts

Abstract This chapter deals with the application of Islamic commercial contracts as they are applied in modern day Islamic finance. Due to the complexities of modern ay financial landscape, the contracts that were developed and elaborated by Muslim jurists of the past are moulded to a greater extent in order to make them applicable in the modern world. This has resulted in the emergence innovative application of the classical Islamic law contracts in contemporary Islamic finance. Thus, we find that the famously found in Islamic law like murabahah, musharakah, mudharabah, ijarah, salam, and istisna etc., are usually applied in a group form. Similarly, these contracts are designed in novel ways in order to fulfil the needs of the modern day finance. Thus, this chapter elaborates the application of the classical Islamic contracts in the modern day Islamic finance with the help of diagrams and illustrations.

Keywords Contracts · Murabahah · Ijarah · Salam · Musharakah · Mudharabah

Introduction

As discussed in the previous chapter, there is a bunch of contracts as well as trade practices that have been disapproved by Islamic commercial law. However, there are also contracts which are deemed permissible

M. Ali and N. Zada, *The Islamic Finance Trading Framework*,
Palgrave CIBFR Studies in Islamic Finance,
https://doi.org/10.1007/978-3-319-96613-7_3

by Shariah and such contracts have been used in the Muslim societies throughout the centuries. However, the last century saw a revolution in the development of Islamic commercial law and the contracts approved by this law. Thus, we see that the contracts permissible under Islamic law are now adopted and molded in a variety of forms. This is due to the differences between the situation when these contracts were developed through centuries and the drastic changes that have taken place in the sphere of business and finance during the last century or so. Consequently, we find that contemporary Muslim scholars have primarily responded positively to these changes by allowing these traditionally approved contracts to be applied in the modern context within the parameters deemed permissible by Shariah. A significant step in this connection is the combination of different contracts which has enabled Islamic law to come up with the required business and finance structures deemed necessary to cater for the needs of the modern-day needs. These and many other efforts have enabled Islamic financial institutions to present themselves as a practical solution provider to the modern-day demands. Although some critics have raised concern about these developments, it is hardly deniable that contemporary Islamic finance which is founded on the grounds of classical Islamic commercial law has provided a fresh air among the prevailing conventional financial systems.

This brings us to briefly discuss the issue of combination of contracts in Islamic commercial. As mentioned in the previous chapter, particular types of combinations are prohibited, like the combination of sale with loan contract. However, a great majority of contracts' combinations do not form part of this prohibition when certain conditions are observed in the process of combination. This flexibility has helped the contemporary Islamic finance greatly. Consequently, there is hardly any contract legalized in Islamic law which is used as a standalone contract to design a product. It is always the outcome of a bunch of these contracts that they form a compatible financial instrument. The issue of combination of contracts is so important that the Accounting and Auditing Organization for Islamic Financial Institutions (AAOIFI) issued its standard no. 25 in 2010 elaborating the rules that should be observed while combining more than one contracts in a transaction. Hasan (2014) has summarized the AAOIFI standard on combination in the following points:

- Combining should not include the case that Shariah explicitly bars. For example, a sale and lending cannot be part of the same set.

- The combination cannot be used as a trick to introduce riba by the backdoor, for example, when two parties may practice bay al-'inah even though it is allowed in Malaysia under restriction.
- Combining should not be used as an excuse for riba taking. For example, A buys a book from B for $100 today on the promise that B will buy back the book for $120 a year later. The literature quotes such cases from the thirteenth-century practices in the Muslim lands.
- Combined contracts should not reveal a disparity or contradiction with regard to their underlying rulings and ultimate goals. Examples of contradictory contracts include granting as asset to someone as a gift and selling or leasing it to the person simultaneously (p. 147).

In this chapter, we present an overview of the famous commercial contracts that are allowed under Islamic law. The classification and division of these contracts have already been explained in the previous chapter. Here, the focus is on the main terms and conditions as well as the practical application of these contracts in human life in general and in the field of contemporary Islamic finance in particular. The contracts discussed in this chapter include murabahah, salam, istisna, ijarah, wakalah, mudharabah, musharakah, bay al-sarf, and rahn as follows.

Murabahah

The root word from which murabahah is derived is ribh which means gain or profit. Thus, murabahah is a sale contract in which the seller earns a profit margin over and above the cost price. For a murabahah sale to take place, it is mandatory that the seller must disclose the cost price so that the buyer is aware of the profit that he is paying above this price. This contract has become the most favorite of the Islamic financial institutions and needs special attention.

Murabahah is also called cost-plus-sale (Al-Zuhayli, 2007) or cost-plus-profit contract (Çizakça, 2011). For a sale to constitute murabahah, some conditions need to be met first. The initial price should be known because it is not possible to add a profit to it if it is unknown. Similarly, the profit margin should also be known because murabahah belongs to the category of trust sales, whereby the buyer consents to pay a specific amount of profit to the seller on the basis of information provided to him by the later. Likewise, the initial price for which the seller bought the item should be fungible so that the cost and profit added to the cost are both known (Al-Zuhayli, 2007).

It is noteworthy that the initial price of a murabahah sale also includes extra costs incurred by the seller. For instance, if the seller bought an item for 100 but then paid 20 more for its delivery, the price will be counted as 120. Therefore, selling this item for 150 will mean that the profit margin is 30.

A simple murabahah structure with its process flow is presented in Fig. 3.1:

1. The first buyer (who is also the second seller) purchases an item from the first seller. This sale is on either cash basis or deferred basis.
2. The first buyer pays the price of the purchased item to the first seller, either on deferred basis or on cash basis as the case may be.

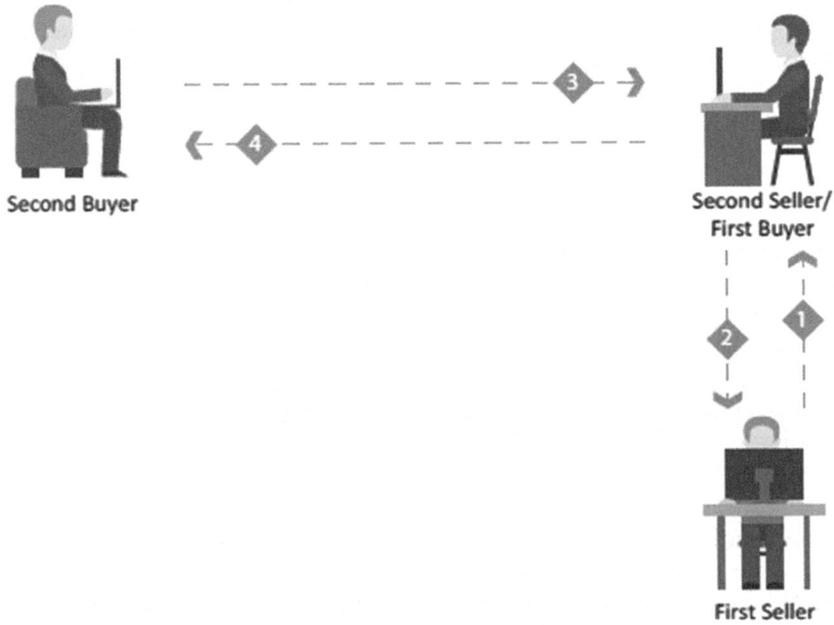

Fig. 3.1 Ordinary *murābaḥah* structure

However, if he is to pay on deferred basis, he must inform the second buyer that his purchase of the item from the first seller was on deferred basis.

3. The first buyer/second seller then sells the item to the second buyer. He also discloses the cost price to the second buyer, further explaining whether the first sale was on cash or deferred basis.

The second buyer pays the price to the second seller either on deferred basis or on cash basis (ISRA, 2016, p. 213).

In its classical dimension, murabahah contract was envisaged to be used in a particular situation. If a consumer is not shrewd, he may be charged a huge profit margin by a skilled seller. Therefore, the disclosure of original cost price by the seller will satisfy the buyer with respect to the profit earned charged to him. However, due to the close proximity of a murabahah sale with the conventional debt-based loan mechanism, a murabahah contract can be used to create a deferred debt with the desired profit margin. This is what has led to the increased popularity of this mode of financing in the Islamic finance industry.

It is pertinent to mention that murabahah in its classical form need not be a credit sale as it can also be a spot transaction. However, it is due to the nature of banks and other financial institutions that currently murabahah has become an equivalent to credit sale. In its simple form, an Islamic bank would buy a commodity from vendor on cash price and would sell the same to its customer after adding its profit margin to it. Thus, the customer receives the commodity it is looking for, while the Islamic bank gets paid in installments like a simple financing contract in a conventional bank.

Traditionally, it was envisioned by the forefathers of Islamic banks that equity-based contract including musharakah and mudharabah will be the foundation of Shariah compliant banking. However, murabahah was approved initially to kick-start the system with the aim to shift gradually toward risk-sharing and equity-based contract. But things did not go as expected. Even when Islamic banking is approaching its golden jubilee in less than a decade, murabahah has become *the norm* with a meager share of equity-based contracts. This demands an inquiry into this state of affairs.

Due to the fact that most Islamic bankers have an academic and practical background in conventional banking and finance, they find murabahah to be most aligned and fit structure to the conventional banking system.

The risk level in a murabahah transaction is akin to a debt contract in conventional banks which makes this contract an eye apple for Islamic banks. The regulatory risk treatment endorses this idea. Additionally, this mode of financing is also free from the moral hazard issue associated with equity-based contracts. Furthermore, the risk-averse nature of banking industry is also adding to this trend. Risk-sharing is said to be a feature of the capital markets while banks are deemed as providing safety and security of the depositors' funds by undertaking as little risk as possible.

Likewise, equity-based contract also suffers from the issue of agency problem. In fact, equity-based Islamic banking was tested at few places but the experiment did not succeed because in both musharakah and mudharabah has no say while the customer can claim losses in the venture. This leaves an Islamic bank with no resort but to bear the losses, a situation that is skilfully handled under a murabahah contract because after the sale of the commodity to the customer, the Islamic banks can retain the ownership of the sold commodity as pledge until all the outstanding balance is paid by the customer. These are some of the factors that make murabahah the most favorite contract of Islamic banks today.

Thus, murabahah today is the most favorite contract of Islamic banks on both their liability and asset side, especially the later side. Customer can deposit money with these banks and can also get financing through murabahah. A simple example should suffice to explain the point. A customer needs to buy a car. She approached an Islamic bank and makes a request for this purpose. After the procedure is followed, the Islamic bank buys a car from a dealer on spot basis and then sells it to the customer, after adding its profit margin to it, on deferred basis. The customer pays the price in installments.

Salam

In simple words, salam can be described as forward sale in which one party pays the price for an item in advance while its delivery is deferred to a specific date in the future. If a person needs some fungible item in the future, he may pay for it today in order to get a discount for early payment. Similarly, a person who will get something in ownership in the future may need cash today. This is especially true in some cases like farming, whereby the farmers need cash to buy the things (seed, fertilizer, etc.) needed for farming. Thus, salam fulfills the needs of both the parties.

Recalling our discussion in the previous about the prohibited elements in Islamic commercial law, one should logically expect salam contract to be banned by Shariah. This is because the item of sale is currently not in the possession and ownership of the seller. In fact, the item of sale may not even exist at the time of sale and this is a form of uncertainty or gharar which is prohibited by Shariah. However, this contract has been explicitly declared legal by the Prophet (SAW) and the Muslim scholars are unanimous on its permissibility. The ambiguity or uncertainty is removed by a detailed description of the item of sale. The logic for the permissibility of salam contract is said to be the need of the masses for such mechanism.

Just like other permissible sale contracts in Islamic commercial law, salam should also fulfill all the requirements of a legal sale under Islamic law. However, there are extra conditions for salam contract too. These conditions pertain to both the price and object of salam. The most important condition for the validity of salam contract pertaining to its price is that the price should be paid in advance. This is understandable because the object of salam is already deferred, and if even the price is deferred, it would lead to the sale of two liabilities which is not permissible under Shariah rules. However, since the price in salam is paid in advance, it is the object of salam that needs to fulfill extra important conditions including the following.

The genus of the item, i.e., whether it is wheat or barley, should be known. Also, its type should also be known. Additionally, its characteristics should also clearly be specified, just as its amount should be made known via volume, number, weight, or size. Next, the price and the item should not be such that belongs to the category of ribawi items. These are six items including gold, silver, wheat, dates, salt, and barley. Thus, condition is put because the ruling for the exchange of such items is that it should be hand in hand. Additionally, the item should be such that it can be identified by specification. Likewise, the item should be such that it should exist and be easily available in the market at the time of delivery. It is pertinent to note that option is not available in a salam contract and it is binding on the parties if the salam object is delivered by the seller as per the specification. The place where the item is to be delivered should also be known (Al-Zuhayli, 2007). Thus, it is evident that these detailed conditions remove the gharar in salam contract and make it permissible in the eyes of Shariah.

The application of salam contract in modern Islamic banking can be understood in Fig. 3.2:

1. A farmer enters into a salam contract with an Islamic bank to sell a specified amount of wheat to be delivered on a specific future date for a fixed price.
2. The price of wheat is paid by the Islamic bank to the farmer on spot basis.
3. The bank also enters into a promise with another customer B, whereby the customer undertakes to purchase the wheat from bank that is to be delivered to it on the future date.
4. Once the farmer supplied the wheat to Islamic bank on the specific date, the bank informs customer B to execute sale contract and take delivery of the wheat (ISRA, 2016, p. 225).

Due to the diverse nature of the demands of customers, Islamic banks have found salam contract very useful for some products and situations. For instance, these banks may want to finance farmers for which salam is the most suitable contract, whereby the Islamic banks provide financing to farmers and buy their produce from them in advance. However, since Islamic banks do not really need the produce which will be delivered to them in the future, they need to dispose these as well. This is

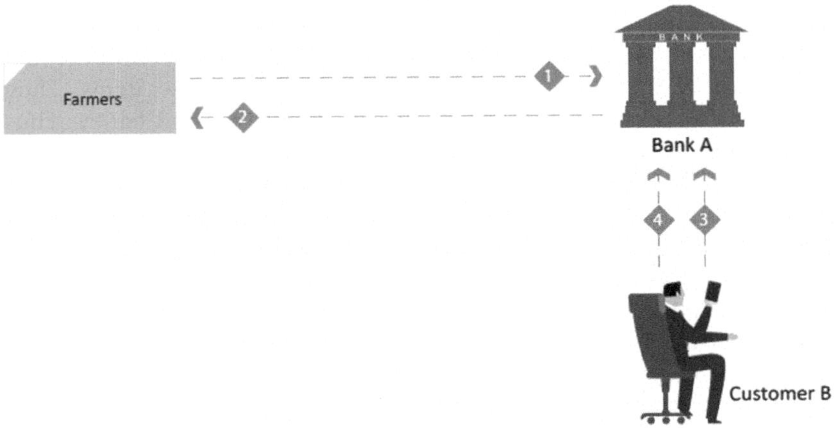

Fig. 3.2 Application of the *salam* contract in agricultural financing

where salam proves very helpful. On the one hand, Islamic banks enter into a salam contract with farmers and buy their produce in advance. On the other hand, they enter into a second or parallel salam contract with potential buyers of such produce. The banks keep the marginal difference between the two salam contracts as their profit.

Istisna

Istisna is the contract of manufacturing which shares many features with salam contract just as the two are unique in certain ways. In fact, some jurists consider the two as the same. However, there are some differences between the two as we shall explain soon. Like salam, istisna is a sale contract in which something that does not exist is the subject matter of the contract. For instance, a customer orders a carpenter to make a bed of specific features for the orderer; this is where istisna is different from salam because salam does not involve manufacturing. Hence, the contract is concluded on something that does not even exist at the time of concluding the contract. Once the object is manufactured, the two parties need to renew the offer and acceptance and the sale takes place eventually.

The need for istisna contract is clear. There are certain professionals in every society that have the skill to manufacture different types of items required by masses in a society. Such objects do not exist initially and it is the effort, skill, and time of these professionals that bring these items into existence. To do so, these skilled persons may need to be instructed in advance just as they may need to be financed in order to arrange the raw material for this purpose. This is where istisna plays its role in fulfilling the needs of both the manufacturers and those who want items manufactured by them.

There are specific conditions unique to the nature of istisna contract. Both the raw material required to make the item and the labor required for it should be arranged by the manufacturer. However, it is not a condition for istisna that the manufacturer makes the object himself; he can hire someone for this purpose, or even order someone else to perform the task. Similarly, istisna is only possible in those objects that can be manufactured and which can be identified by specification. Therefore, it cannot be done in items like fruit, animals, and corn because these items are not manufacturer. It is possible in items like buildings, bridges, and the like. Similarly, istisna can be concluded to make items that are unique or homogenous. Hasan (2014, p. 145) has outlined the requirements of an istisna contract as follows:

- The item to be delivered must be clearly specified in terms of its nature, quality, and measurements.
- The manufacturer (builder) must make a commitment to produce the item as per the description and specifications.
- The manufacturer (builder) is to deliver the item upon the completion of its production without needing a fix completion date.
- The contract cannot be revoked once the production process has started except where items are found to be not meeting the specifications as per the agreement.
- The payment can be made in installments linked with the progress of the work or in a lump sum before or after the time of delivery.
- The manufacturer (builder) alone is responsible for obtaining the inputs needed for the completion of the production process.
- The manufacturer (builder) cannot assume the role of a financial intermediary between the buyer and the third party, especially if the buyer has become unable to meet the obligations toward such a third party.

A simple explanation of istisna contract in its classical framework is presented in Fig. 3.3:

1. A customer approaches a manufacturer and requests him to manufacture a specific item for him which is to be delivered on a specific date, at a price agreed by both which is to be paid at an agreed date in the future or on spot.

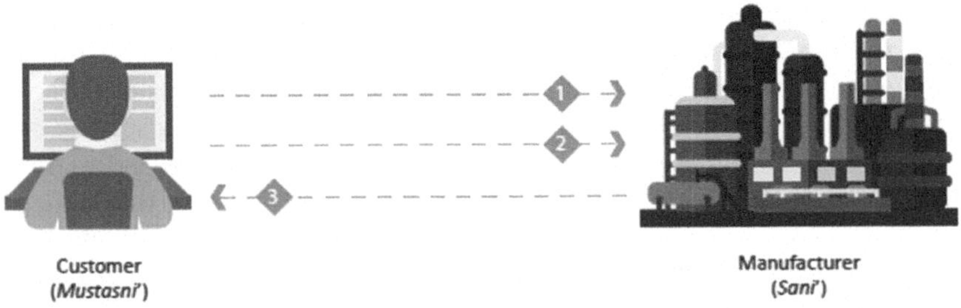

Fig. 3.3 Classical istisna structure

2. The customer accordingly pays the price to the manufacturer either on cash or on deferred/installment basis.
3. Once the asset is completed, it is delivered by the manufacturer to the customer on the stipulated date (ISRA, 2016, p. 219).

Istisna is practiced in Islamic banks currently. This contract is especially suitable for the making of buildings and other projects such as bridges, highways, ships, and the like. In fact, this contract suits the purpose of infrastructure and project financing. Therefore, if a customer needs a house, for example, it can be built by the Islamic bank under the contract of istisna. However, just like salam contract, the Islamic bank will need to find a party which can construct the object on its behalf for the customer because the banks do not perform such duties. Therefore, a parallel istisna is signed by the Islamic bank with another party, whereby the Islamic bank asks that party to construct the house as per the requirement and description provided by the client. After the completion of the construction, the Islamic bank takes the house into its ownership followed by its sale/delivery to the client.

Ijarah

Like all other types of sale contract, the contract of ijarah or lease has been discussed in detail in Islamic commercial law. It follows all the general conditions and requirements of a sale contract, just as it has its own specific conditions and requirements that need to be observed. The essence of this contract is the sale of usufruct against compensation or rent. Like salam and istisna contracts, ijarah is the sale of something, i.e., the usufruct, which does not exist at the time of sale but exists in the course of time. According to the majority of the jurists, the subject matter of lease contract can also be the usufruct of an item that is to be made in the future.

The need and rational of a lease contract are evident. One has different types of needs including the need to use the usufruct of an item without having the need to own that item itself. Thus, on the one hand, there are the owners of such items who do not need or want to use such usufruct generating items themselves and on the other hand there are those who need the usufructs of such items only. A lease contract brings these two groups of people together. Those who need to use usufruct get them by paying rent or compensation to the owners of such items.

Examples include the lease of a car, a house, an office, an aeroplane, a piece of machinery, and the like.

In Islamic commercial law, a lease contract has many classification and subsequent types. An ijarah is classified first on the basis of the type of subject matter where it is tangible or intangible (labor). Examples of the first type include the lease of building, land, and office while the second type includes an employee or an independent contractor. Similarly, ijarah can be binding or non-binding. In the first case, neither of the two parties keeps the option of inspection, defect, or stipulation for themselves. If any of these are retained by any of the parties to ijarah, the contract becomes non-binding until the expiry of the option period (ISRA, 2016). A simple lease contract of a moveable asset is presented in Fig. 3.4:

1. The lessor leases a house/car, etc., to the lessee for a specific rental amount.
2. The lessee pays the rental as per the terms of the agreement, and at the end of the lease period, the lessee returns the leased asset back to the lessor (Saleem, 2013, p. 57).

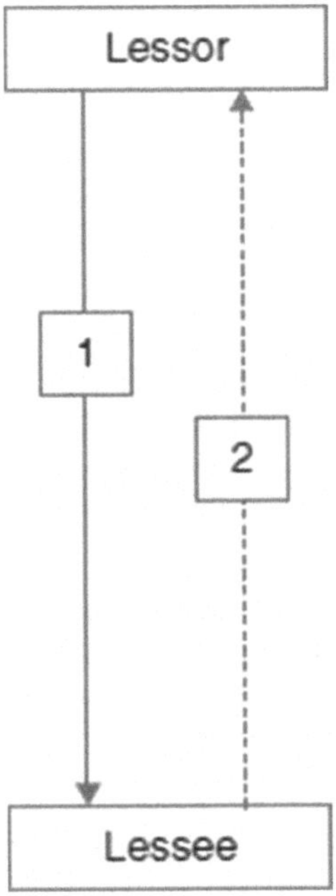

Fig. 3.4 Lease of a moveable asset

Apart from the general sale conditions, there are specific conditions required for a lease contract to be legally valid under Islamic law. Some of the important conditions include the following.

The lease object should be properly known so as to avoid any disputes arising in the future. There are three dimensions pertaining to the knowledge of the object of lease:

1. Knowledge of the type of benefit or usufruct to be derived from the object,
2. Knowledge of the period of the lease, and
3. Knowledge of the nature of labor in leasing the labor of skilled or unskilled workers (Al-Zuhayli, 2007, p. 391).

Due to the nature of ijarah contract, it is important that the object of lease should be such that they can be hired or utilized but their substance of corpus remains unconsumed. Therefore, currency, fuel, cotton, edible, ammunition, and candles cannot be leased because they perish after utilization. Likewise, it is also not permissible to lease one item in compensation for another item of similar genus like house for house.

The famous Muslim jurist al-Kasani has mentioned many conditions for the validity of ijarah contract which are summarized below:

- The contracted usufruct has to be ascertained to avoid any dispute.
- The lease period must be specified. However, in the case of a wage/service, any of the two, i.e., the amount of work or the time period for a job should be known.
- Benefiting from the hired goods should be possible. As such, lease of a nonexistent asset for usufruct of which a description cannot be determined precisely is not allowed, because such gharar about the description and the time may lead to disputes. In other words, the purpose of the contract must be capable of being fulfilled and performed.
- The handing over/delivery of the contracted goods for taking their benefit is essential. No rent becomes due merely because of execution of the contract, unless the subject of the lease is delivered and made available to the lessee. However, advance rent can be taken when availability is ensured for the period of the lease.
- In the case of workmen or service, the contracting person should be capable of undertaking the job. Therefore, hiring a runaway animal for riding or usurped assets is invalid.

- The usufruct of contracted goods must be lawful, meaning that the purpose of ijarah should not be unlawful or haram.
- The usufruct should be conventional or according to the tradition of the people (Ayub, 2009, pp. 281–282).

With respect to liability in connection with the leased asset, the liabilities arising out of the ownership will be borne by the lessor or owner of the object. For example, in the case of leasing a house or a care, the owner will be responsible for paying taxes related to the house/car. However, liabilities like paying of electricity/water bills and fuel charges will be borne by the lessee. Similarly, the lessee is not responsible for damages caused to the leased asset unless it is proved that it was caused by the lessee's negligence, misconduct, or breach of terms.

Ijarah contract has great potential and is frequently used in Islamic finance today. There are two types of lease mechanisms used in Islamic banks for the purpose of financing. The first is known as operating lease while the second is called finance lease. Operating lease is not tied to a sale or gift at the end of the lease period. Thus, when the contract expires, the object of lease is returned to the Islamic bank. The terms of this lease are short as compared to the useful life of the asset. The lessor only transfers the right to use the property but retains its legal ownership and the risks associated with such ownership. However, there is a sale or gift contract at the end of finance lease, whereby the item is either sold or gifted to the lessee at the end of the contract. This sale of gift contract is independent of the original lease contract in order to comply with the Shariah restrictions of combination of contracts. According to AAOIFI guidelines, the transfer of ownership to the lessee can take place in either of the three forms:

1. By means of a promise to sell for a token or other consideration, or by accelerating the payment of the remaining amount of rental, or by paying the market value of the leased property.
2. A promise to give it as a *hibah* or gift (for no consideration).
3. A promise to give it as a gift, contingent upon the payment of the remaining installments.

Furthermore, the rental amount in finance lease is higher as compared to operating lease. This is because the rental amount in finance lease is almost equal to the amount paid under installment sale; both installment sale and finance lease have more or less the same economic outcome.

In the sphere of Islamic capital market, ijarah sukuk, the Shariah compliant alternative to conventional bonds, is a very famous instrument. Under normal ijarah sukuk structure, a special purpose vehicle (SPV) established by the entity that needs to raise funds is formed which issues sukuk to the investors and raises funds from them. Next, the SPV purchases an asset from a supplier and leases it to the entity. The entity uses the asset and makes rental payment which is distributed among the sukuk investors periodically. At the end of the contract, the entity purchases the asset from the SPV pursuant to a purchase undertaking given by the entity. The sukuk investors are paid back their initial investment.

Wakalah

The word wakalah has several meanings including delegation, authorization, or performing a task on behalf of another. In its standard no. 23, AAOIFI defined wakalah as the act of one party delegating the other to act on its behalf in what can be a subject matter of delegation. Thus, wakalah is a contract in which the principal (called muwakkil) authorizes a party as his agent (called wakil) to perform tasks on his behalf (ISRA, 2016).

Wakalah is a non-binding contract by nature, and therefore, any of the two parties can withdraw from it by mutual agreement, unilateral termination, or discharge of the obligation. Additionally, wakalah can be paid or voluntary. Hence, the principal will be required to pay the agent if they agreed it to be so. Similarly, wakalah can be general or restricted. In general wakalah, the principal asks the agent to perform a specific task, e.g., buy a house, without specifying any further detail. But in restricted wakalah, he restricts the buying of house with, for instance, a particular price. Similarly, wakalah can be restricted to a certain period of time. But it can also be left unrestricted with respect to time if the two parties agreed (ISRA, 2016). It is the responsibility of the agent to perform all delegated tasks as per the instructions of the principal and exercise due care and diligence in the process. Any action performed by the agent on behalf of the principal with due diligence will be deemed an action by the principal (Ayub, 2009).

A particular type of agency has been recognized under Islamic law known as fadhuli or unauthorized agent. It is a person who involves in the matters of others without concern. It is a type of contract in which one person acts on behalf of another without prior authorization.

According to the most preferred opinion, this contract is valid but pending the approval of the principal (Saleem, 2013). If approved, it will have a retrospective effect and all right and liabilities of an agency contract will come into effect from the time of concluding the unauthorized act.

Like other sale contracts, the general conditions of a sale contract pertaining to the parties, the expression, and the subject matter, there are other important conditions to be found in wakalah including, but not limited to the following:

- The principal should know the agent, either by name or by his physical appearance. Likewise, the agent should identify his principal either by name or by his characteristics.
- The rights and responsibilities of the transaction entered into by the agent shall lie with the agent, such as taking possession and delivery of the purchased asset.
- However, if the agent attributes the transaction to the principal, the rights and responsibilities of the transaction shall lie with the principal.
- The agent as trustee shall not be liable in the event of loss or damage of the asset except if such loss or damage is caused by his misconduct, negligence, or breach of specified terms.
- If the agent is given remuneration for the provided service, the Shariah ruling of ijarah shall apply (ISRA, 2016, p. 262).

Wakalah is frequently used in different Islamic finance contracts. In fact, there is hardly an instrument where wakalah is missing. Even in a simple murabahah transaction, the client is appointed as wakil by the Islamic bank to purchase the asset on the bank's behalf. But wakalah has gained specific importance as Islamic finance is advancing further. The concept of wakalah bi al-istithmar or investment agency is becoming increasingly popular, especially in the sphere of sukuk. Under this mechanism, as elaborated by Ayub (2009), the Islamic financial institutions manage funds of the investors on the basis of agency. They manage these funds on agency basis and charge a pre-agreed fee for their services irrespective of the profit or loss of the respective portfolio. The fee can be charged in different possible ways: It can be a part of the percentage of investment amount on monthly or annual remuneration basis, or it can be fixed in a lump sum. However, it is necessary to determine one of these mechanisms before the launch of the fund.

The structure of wakalah bi al-istithmar or investment agency contract is explained in Fig. 3.5:

1. According to the agency agreement, the investor appoints the Islamic bank as its investment agent.
2. The bank invests the money as per the terms of the agency agreement.
3. The investor receives the expected returns as well as the principal amount at the end of the contract.
4. If there are any surplus returns, they are either shared by the investors and Islamic bank, or given to the bank as incentive fee.
5. In the event of bank's negligence, the principal is returned to the investor along with waiver of wakalah fee and/or compensation (ISRA, 2016, pp. 274–275).

In the Islamic capital market, wakalah sukuk are becoming increasingly popular. Under a plain wakalah bil istithmar sukuk, the principals (sukuk investors) appoint an agent to invest the former's capital in order to

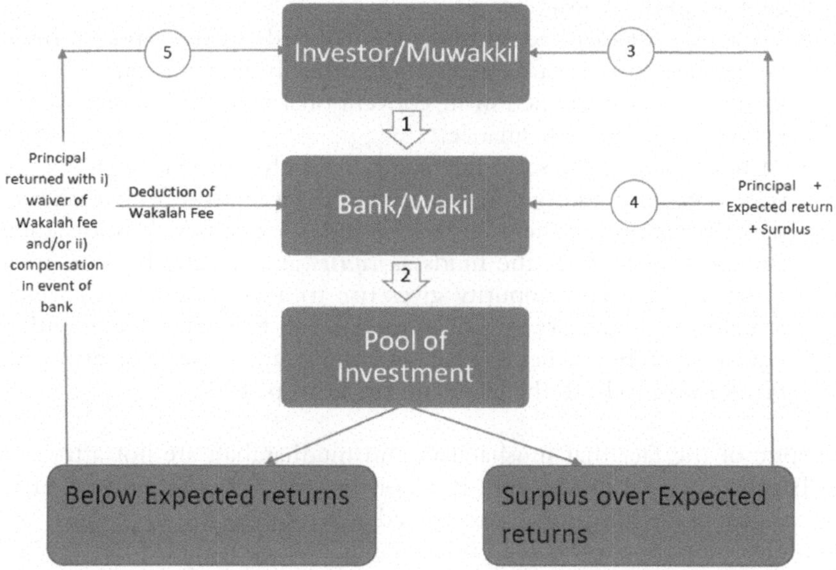

Fig. 3.5 Basic structure of a fee-based wakalah bi al-istithmar contract

generate profits. The agent charges a fee for its services. The risk of the acquisition and investment is borne by the principals. Similarly, they are entitled to any profits generated from the investment activities.

Musharakah

Both musharakah and mudharabah constitute the participatory or risk-sharing-based modes of financing. As discussed earlier in this chapter, these modes were initially proposed to be the backbone of modern Islamic finance. Unlike debt-based financing, equity-based or risk-sharing-based financing ensures equity and justice among the parties concerned, and they are more akin to the realization of the higher objectives of Shariah. Currently, these two modes are, however, not in the good books of Islamic financial institutions and there are certain reasons for it as explained by Hasan (2014) in the following three points:

- Social dynamics, cultural patterns, and demographic explosion over the centuries eroded the personal intimacy and trust on which participatory finance flourished unabated till the close of the thirteenth century in the Muslim world.
- There was a lack of adequate legal safeguards to the capital providers against loss, including discrimination in allowing interest payments as a cost deduction in conventional lending but not of the profit share in Islamic finance.
- At both ends of the scale—demand or supply—mudharabah finance is neither pure equity nor pure debt. It is a mixture which takes in part the features of them both. It would, for example, be misleading for the firm to treat the funds as ***equity*** and for the bank to treat them as ***debt***. This impurity gives rise to agency confusion, which arguably can be more serious in mudarabah financing than in either equity or debt financing, making mudharabah the least attractive proposition to both the bank and the firm (p. 120).

In spite of the fact that musharakah and mudharabah are not attractive to Islamic financial institutions, it is not deniable that the industry players continuously long for a widespread use of these modes. These are thought to be the way forward if Islamic finance ever wants to achieve its dreams of social justice and equity.

The word musharakah from the root word sharikah linguistically refers to mixing of two properties in such a way that defining the separate parts is no more possible; it also means sharing and participation. Technically, it is defined by jurists as a contract between a group of individuals who share the capital and profits. The wisdom in permitting partnership is that it allows the partners mix their properties in such a way that leads to generating maximum benefit than could be generated individually (Al-Zuhayli, 2007).

There are two broad types of partnerships discussed in Islamic commercial law: general partnership and contractual partnership. In general partnership, there is very little flexibility for the partners as compared to the second category (Al-Zuhayli, 2007). In general partnership, two or more persons become joint owner of a property without entering into a formal partnership contract. There are two ways in which such partnership could be established: by operation of law or via a contract (other than partnership contract). Example of the first type includes inheritance while bequeath and gift are examples of the second type (Saleem, 2013). General partnership is further divided into voluntary and involuntary. Voluntary general partnership is established as a result of joint purchase or joint receivership of gifts or bequests accepted by partners, whereas involuntary general partnerships are formed without an act of approval by the partners like the automatic inheritance of property by the heirs (Al-Zuhayli, 2007). Contractual partnership, on the other hand, is defined as a contract between two or more partners, whereby they agree to partner in the capital and profit. Since the parties concerned willingly enter into a contractual arrangement for joint investment and sharing of subsequent profits and losses, it is considered as the proper type of partnership (Saleem, 2013) and it can also be termed as "joint commercial enterprise" (ISRA, 2016). This is the type that concerns us in this section.

Contractual partnership is further divided into the following four types:

1. Partnership in capital: In this type of partnership, all the partners contribute capital into the business venture. This type of partnership is further divided into two types: general and equal. Under equal partnership, the contributed capital, debt liability, and mutual responsibility are equally shared by each partner. In general

partnership, on the other hand, such equality is not required and this type is most akin to the modern concept of business partnership.

2. Partnership in services/labor: This is a partnership agreement between two or more parties to provide a service jointly and share the profit from the work as per the agreed-upon ratio. There is no capital contribution required in monetary form for this type of partnership.
3. Partnership in goodwill: Under this type of partnership, the partners enter into partnership on the basis of their goodwill and creditworthiness. They buy assets on credit on the basis of their creditworthiness for the purpose of making profit. The percentage of profit and liability sharing is determined by the partners mutually.
4. Partnership in profit: This type is famously known by mudharabah which stands for capital contribution from one partner and labor from the other. The profit earned is shared between the two as per agreed ratio while losses are borne by the capital provider. This type will be discussed in detail later.

Like other contracts discussed previously in this chapter, there are general conditions required for a partnership contract to be valid. As discussed in the previous chapters, these conditions relate to the contracting parties, the expression of the contract and the subject matter and price of contract. Additionally, some other requirements for a partnership contract include the following:

- The ratio of profit sharing among the partners should be fixed at the time of concluding the contract. However, this ratio cannot be a fixed amount; rather, it has to be a specific percentage of the expected profit earned. This is important in order to avoid disputes and gharar as no profits may be realized from the venture.
- It is permissible to have profit-sharing ratio which is not proportionate to the capital contributed by the partners. However, a sleeping partner, i.e., a partner that is not taking part in the business management, cannot have a share of profit more than his capital contribution.
- Losses can only be shared as per the capital contribution.
- Although the capital of partnership should be in monetary form, the jurists allow to contribute tangible assets as the capital of

partnership provided that all partners agree to it and that the monetary value of these assets is determined.
- Not all the partners are required to participate in the management of the business.

It has been discussed previously why musharakah is not very famous among Islamic banks. However, this contract is still used to a certain degree. Of particular importance is a unique type of partnership called musharakah mutanaqisah or diminishing musharakah. In diminishing musharakah, the Islamic bank enters into partnership contract with a potential buyer to buy an item. Thus, the two become owners of the said item. Afterward, the Islamic bank leases its portion of the bought item to the customer and the customer pays monthly rental for this. However, the customer simultaneously buys a small portion of the bank's share in the item on frequent basis which leads to a decrease in the ownership of the bank in the said item. With the passage of time, the share of the bank decreases, a situation denoted by the term "diminishing," until it is wholly bought by the customer who becomes the ultimate owner of the item.

The structure of musharakah mutanaqisah home financing is presented in Fig. 3.6:

1. A house which is already completed is bought by a customer who also pays a deposit of 10% of the price.
2. Next, the customer enters into a musharakah mutanaqisah contract with the Islamic bank.
3. The Islamic bank pays the remaining 90% of the price to the house developer. The bank, thus, becomes the owner of the 90% shares of the house.
4. The Islamic bank then leases its 90% share in the house to the customer who pays rental to the bank on monthly basis.
5. Each month, the customer pays the monthly rental but also buys a small share of the property from the Islamic bank until he becomes the owner of the 100% shares of the house at the end of the contract tenure (ISRA, 2016, p. 263).

Like Islamic banking, musharakah sukuk is also not among the favorite instruments in Islamic capital market. However, musharakah sukuk are found in the market. A musharakah sukuk represents undivided ownership of the sukuk holders in the business venture. Normally, this sukuk is

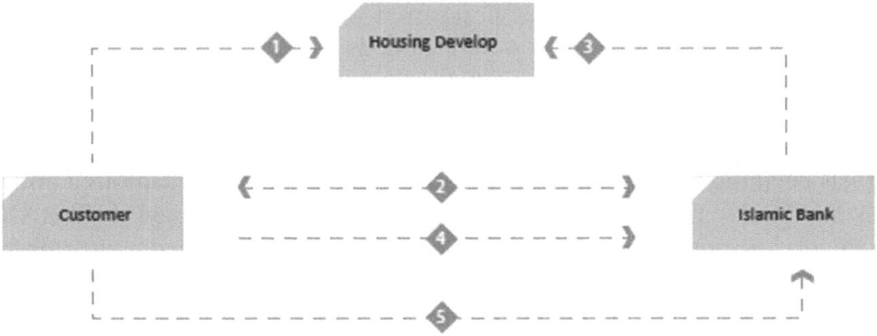

Fig. 3.6 Musharakah mutanaqisah structure for home financing

issued to undertake a specific project or to have a stake in the business of the issuer. Accordingly, the funds raised from sukuk investors are injected into the issuer's business or project. The return from the venture is then distributed between them as per the agreement. At the end of the term, the issuer purchases the portion of the sukuk investors in the venture and they get their money in full.

Mudharabah

As defined in the previous discussion on musharakah, mudharabah is a type of partnership in which capital is contributed by one party while the skill and labor are added from another party. Based on this structure, mudharabah is also called silent partnership. The main difference between a mudharabah and musharakah is that in musharakah, all the partners can partake in the management of the venture. Similarly, another distinguishing feature is the bearing of losses; in mudharabah, all the losses are to be borne by the capital provider while the entrepreneur only loses his effort and time. It is also a requirement for mudharabah that the capital contributor (known as rabb al-maal) should refrain from interfering into the venture management by the entrepreneur. Mudharabah is also called qiradh and muqaradhah by some jurists.

A simple process flow of mudharabah is presented in Fig. 3.7:

1. Rabb al-mall (also known as sahib al-maal) contributes the capital to the business project.
2. The mudharib contributes his efforts to the business project.

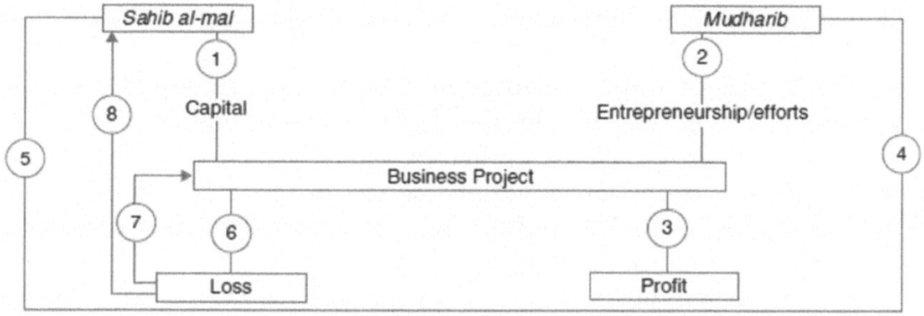

Fig. 3.7 Mudharabah process flow

3. As a result of business activities undertaken by the mudharib, profits are generated.
4. Mudharib receives his share from the profit generated.
5. The sahib al-mall similarly receives his portion of profit.
6. However, it may be the case that losses are incurred in the process.
7. In the case of losses, they are offset by the profit from the business.
8. However, in case the losses are more than profit, they are borne by the sahib al-mal while the mudharib loses in the form of his efforts gone unrewarded (Saleem, 2013, p. 112).

The practice of mudharabah was prevalent even in the pre-Islamic Arabia. Even the Prophet Muhammad (SAW) worked as mudharib at a young age. It is also argued by many that this structure was later on exported to some parts of Europe. In any case, mudharabah is a perfect structure where a person is skilled but does not have the required capital to utilize his skills in doing business. Similarly, it fits the needs of a capitalist with no business skills or no time to do business. The two parties can reap the benefits of their respective strengths by partnering under the contract of mudharabah.

Mudharabah is of two types: restricted and unrestricted. In restricted mudharabah, the capital provider puts some restrictions on the entrepreneur regarding the management and use of funds. For instance, he may be restricted about the types and/or period of investment, location of investment, as well as the use of funds or any restrictions that the capital provider deems appropriate. On the other hand, there are no such restrictions in unrestricted mudharabah and the entrepreneur enjoys freedom in all these aspects.

Some specific conditions of mudharabah contract are given below:

- The capital of mudharabah should be in cash or liquid form. It should not be in kind in the form of commodities and goods because of the fluctuation in their prices.
- The amount of capital should be known.
- Similarly, the capital should be present. Therefore, a debt cannot be made the capital of mudharabah.
- The capital should be delivered to the mudharib to enable him to do business with it which is the purpose of such venture.
- The capital provider has the right to appoint more than one entrepreneur in which case they both will utilize the capital jointly.
- One entrepreneur can also be hired/appointed by many capital providers.
- The losses will be borne by the capital provider and the entrepreneur will not be liable for these except in the case of misconduct, negligence, and breach of terms.
- A mudharib should exercise due diligence and care in the management of the business venture.
- The liability of the capital provider is restricted to the capital he has contributed. Therefore, an entrepreneur should not incur liabilities greater than the capital except with the explicit permission of capital provider to do so.

In contemporary Islamic finance, mudharabah is normally used on the liability side of the Islamic banks. A customer wanting to deposit with these banks opens account on mudharabah basis. This mudharabah is usually unrestricted because the Islamic bank has the freedom to invest it as mudharib as per its discretion. Any profit earned from the investment is shared as per the agreed ratio while losses are borne by the account holder. The Islamic banks acting as entrepreneurs invest the funds further on mudharabah basis or on the basis of other Shariah compatible modes of financing. In the first case, the mechanism is called two-tier mudharabah; there are two mudharabah transactions in this scenario: the first one between the fund depositor and the Islamic bank (where the Islamic bank acts as entrepreneur) and the second one between the Islamic bank and the financier (where the Islamic bank acts as capital provider). While the use of two-tier mudharabah in Islamic banking seems appreciable at surface, it has been criticized by many due to the fact that Islamic banks keep themselves on the safe ground by transferring the losses to the original capital provider (depositor of fund) while they share the profits with him.

Apart from Islamic banking, mudharabah is also utilized in Islamic capital market in the form of mudharabah sukuk, though it is less frequently used. Under a mudharabah sukuk, the investors (sukuk holders) enter into a mudharabah agreement (via purchasing of mudharabah sukuk) with the issuer (mudharib) to invest in a Shariah compliant business. The issuer uses the funds raised for the specific venture and the income generated from the venture is distributed periodically among the two as per the agreement. At the end of the venture tenure, the issuer purchases back the sukuk via a purchase undertaking and the sukuk are deemed, thereby enabling the sukuk investors to get back their initial investment.

Bay Al-Sarf

Bay al-sarf means exchange of money for money. This includes the exchange of currency, the exchange of gold for gold or silver for silver or gold for silver. This type of sale is permissible in Shariah and it has its own particular conditions that should be met in order for such sale to be valid. The legality and conditions of such sale are derived from a famous Hadith of the Prophet Muhammad (SAW) in which he ordered that gold, silver, wheat, barley, dates, and salt should be exchanged equal and on spot. This Hadith is known as the Hadith of six commodities and the Muslim jurists extended this ruling to other items apart from these six items, like the currency in current times.

The jurists derived certain conditions from this Hadith which should be observed in bay al-sarf. The first condition is that the counter values should be taken in possession before the parties leave each other. Second, the exchange should be equal in terms of weight and/or value. Likewise, it should be on the spot and cannot be deferred to future. These rules also apply to currency exchange. However, the same Hadith allows non-equality in the case when two different items are exchanged, but on the spot exchange is still required. For instance, the exchange or sale of the currency of one country (e.g., US$ versus US$) must be equal and on spot. However, an exchange between two different currencies is allowed to be unequal but it must be on spot still. Deferment is not allowed in either case.

Fig. 3.8 Structure of bay al-sarf in spot forex

The use of bay al-sarf in contemporary Islamic finance is explained in Fig. 3.8:

1. Bank sells a specific currency to the customer and delivers it to him on spot.

The customer pays the price of currency in a different currency on cash basis (ISRA 2016).

References

Al-Zuhayli, W. (2007). *Financial transactions in Islamic jurisprudence* (M. A. el-Gamal, Trans.). Beirut: Dar al-fikir al-Mauaser.

Ayub, M. (2009). *Understanding Islamic finance*. Chichester: Wiley.

Çizakça, M. (2011). *Islamic capitalism and finance: Origins, evolution and the future*. Cheltenham: Edward Elgar.

Hasan, Z. (2014). *Islamic banking and finance: An integrative approach*. Oxford: Oxford University Press.

ISRA. (2016). *Islamic financial system: Principles and operations* (2nd ed.). Kuala Lumpur, Malaysia: International Shari'ah Research Academy for Islamic Finance (ISRA).

Saleem, M. Y. (2013). *Islamic commercial law*. Singapore: Wiley.

CHAPTER 4

Profit-Making in Islam: Justification and Importance

Abstract This chapter discusses profit making in Islam. We also present justification of profit making and why is it an important phenomenon of Islamic trading framework. We argue that in order to construct a well-integrated theory of profit, profit shall be defined revenue minus cost. Secondly, the focal point of the theory shall be a firm instead of an entrepreneur. Additionally, it should be considered as the function of dynamic changes in business environment. Lastly, the profit may be shared between labor and capital in order to endorse fairness, growth, and peace in society. This type of profit theory will be acceptable in both conventional and Islamic trading frameworks.

Keywords Profit · Firm · Entrepreneur · Labor · Capital

Introduction

Islam, a religion that encompasses holistically every aspect of life and a complete code of conduct, respects the human's innate desire to strive for affluence. It does not forbid profit-making, rather encourages its followers to undertake trade as their means of earning and considers the profit as a gift from Almighty Allah. As an innate trait of human nature, profit-making's pervasiveness can be felt in every avenue. Price theory, one of the conventional economics' fundamental theories, is also

M. Ali and N. Zada, *The Islamic Finance Trading Framework*,
Palgrave CIBFR Studies in Islamic Finance,
https://doi.org/10.1007/978-3-319-96613-7_4

centered by profit maximization. Businesses, merchandising, production, and commerce, every notion is insignificant without profit. Despite the immense significance of profit notion, it is yet not highlighted justly in economic theory and other literatures, except for a piece of work by Frank H. Knight's Risk, Uncertainty, and Profit (1921). This unfair negligence is even further in Islamic economics literature.

Islamic economic concept and free entrepreneurship are congruent on many grounds, except for few prohibitions in Islam which are indispensable for society's well-being. The ills of interest, speculation, corruption, and unjust practices, that can lead to grave consequences which today's world economy is facing due to unhampered materialistic drive, are surely forbidden in Islam. Conventional mercantilism has given enough margin to modern commercialism such that present economic scenario is embodiment of disproportional wealth accumulation, poverty elevations, inequality, monopolized power exploitation, and the like. In the name of capitalism and individual freedom, markets tend to overlook the society's welfare. Islam does not, in any respect, disregard freedom of entrepreneurship, individual ownership rights, free rivalry among market's players, and innovativeness. Profit is regarded as pivotal for economic development and wealth generation as in conventional economics.

Many mechanisms and tools have been incorporated into Islamic economic system from past, so as the conception of profit. Therefore, to grasp the Islamic version of profit theory, it would be pertinent to refer the conventional profit theory in a nutshell before elaborating its Islamic form. The later part of the chapter is designed in a manner to well grasp the fundamental arguments pertaining to the conventional concept, afterward forwarding to the issues with respect to the Islamic notion, and finally concluding the subject matter. The aim of the discourse is to well comprehend the Islamic notion of profit and the issues pertain to it.

Profit is not an easy topic to deliberate on. The reason is because profit unlike rent, wages, or interest is not an object in itself. It is simply general category of remaining part of your revenue which if positive will be called profit. As a consequence, discussion on profits raises the range of tricky issues to be addressed.

Issues in Conventional Profit Theory

The exposition of the term "profit" can be expanded into subject areas of its broad definition, how and from where it is derived from, whom it is owned by, and finally how it is accumulated to capital. These issues have been marginally overlooked in the literature body of economics. Therefore, briefly probing into these key queries would be useful to surface the issues pertaining to its Islamic notion.

The conventional economists' view of profit is overly précised and subjective in nature. Concepts like that of depreciation are surfaced on subjective criteria and hence render it marginally biased in nature. Moreover, the inexplicit components, as opportunity costs that are deducted from net profit to come up with the "normal profit," make it ambiguous in nature. The residual of both, net profit and normal profit, is referred to as "economic profit" by the economic theorists. The bifurcation is not as simple as it merely sounds. The inexplicit elements are not easily filtered out to come about with the figure of economic profit.

The sources of profit are explained by the economists with the rudimentary model of unrealistic suppositions. Earlier theories on profit were based on the profitless models but they could not come up with anything concrete. Economists like J. B. Clark discussed it as the function of risk (risk of losing capital). As per Knight, profit is a functional return based on uncertainties faced by the owners of the capital. Schumpeter considered profit as a function of innovation. Hence, economist could not come with a unified theory agreeing on the source of profit.

The field of economics has always considered profit as a return to the entrepreneur for his investment and decision making at the time of uncertainty. As per Knight, being an entrepreneur is something exceptional as an entrepreneur is the one who has the confidence in his judgment coupled with the ability to operationalize the ideas. Additionally, he should be willing to take risk and has capital in his possession. Capital becomes an interesting prerequisite because that enables entrepreneur to employ other factors of production. But in the face of modern forms of business like joint-stock companies where many shareholders pool in their funds but not be making the decisions, Knight's theory does not stand. The decisions are made by specialized functionaries who are salaried individuals. As per Zubair Hasan (1975), the conventional economics couldn't provide any solid theory on profit. On the other hand, an Islamic dispensation which is instilled with ethical values cannot afford such avoidance. Now, we will shift our discussion on how Islam sees profit and we will inspect the Shariah compliant structure of business surpluses.

Islam and Profit

Along with the spiritual insightfulness, Islam honors the worldly thrive of its believers with due respect. Striving for one's livelihood is well acknowledged; rather, trade and business are esteemed when undertaken within the Islamic jurisdictions. The innate human's lust of wealth, if set unbridled, can lead to hazardous consequences. Hence, Islam confines the materialistic ventures of its followers within moral boundaries, with an aim to avoid deprivation of individuals' privileges at any cost, prescribing the ways to earn their appropriate stake. Honesty is the most imperative trait of the business dealings. Either be it the promoting and marketing, or it be the selling of the product to the end customer, honesty can never be overlooked. It is important to the degree that the product's faults also have to be exposed. In Islam, exploiting other's scarce knowledge or false acclaim of one's product for marketing purposes is not legitimate, which the present commerce is embodiment of. One has to prioritize the moral virtues over the voracity of wealth and hence has to act within the Islamic boundaries forgoing the superfluous profit on account of honesty.

These virtuous merits are instilled in believers repeatedly in Quran and Sunnah by emphasizing the comparison between short-termed worldly lives with that of eternal bounties of hereafter, hence cognizing the orderly earnings within Islamic boundaries. The benefit of honesty additionally entails the merits of equity and justice in overall society safeguarding each individual's rights.

One remarkable difference in Islamic economic system from its conventional counterpart is avoiding gharar or speculation. Such activities that include capitalizing on uncertain circumstances entail inherently enormous risk that can trigger devastating consequences cascading to multiple economies around the globe as evidenced from economic crisis. With the strong foundation of justice, equity, honesty, and communal welfare, Islamic economic system disproves the blind hunches for business dealings that can jeopardize the person himself and the counterparties. Hence, the system is indigenously risk mitigating and resilient to deliver a win-win situation for all market players. The inputs to the production process, i.e., land, labor, and capital, are also filtered through Islamic principles to foster Islamic economic system in essence with all its merits and values. Logically, we would further analyze the important issues regarding these factors of production.

Interest in Islam

When Islamic finance or economics is under discussion, the first label it connotes is "interest free." Despite some contradictions, majority of Muslim intellectuals reach an agreement that "riba" is absolutely and entirely prohibited. The consensus pertains to all of its forms and definitions. Regardless of its types, usage, quality, or the underlying contracts, interest is altogether forbidden unanimously. Therefore, rather than reinventing the wheel by jumping into the extensive argument, it is rational to go with the majority and suffice our decision on complete prohibition of interest. When religiously following the Islamic theology, a believer's sufficient reason to abstain from interest is its prohibition in Islam, but when it is projected in literature as a substitute system to conventional economics, Islamic economic system has to be assessed critically as to why interest is prohibited, and how business profit, a quite similar value, is approved while interest not.

One answer to modern economists is from their own economics literature itself. Famous General Theory of Keynes exposed lagging nature of interest rates in comparison with the expected profit, demonstrating inverse behavior with growth and stability. When expected profits tend to be higher than interest rates, inclination of earning through debt increases, consequently leading toward inflation-ridden economic behavior. Reciprocally, when profit expectations tend to fall more steeply than interest rates, the economy faces extending recessionary pattern. Hence, interest brought no good for economic development.

The marginal productivity theory while professing to warrant distributive justice could not justify the interest. Capital (funding) is undeniably important factor of production. Nonetheless, a fundamental question arises that how does interest coincide with productivity? Especially where the main determinants of interest are the market forces in bond markets and the monetary policy rates which are generally set by central bank based on their needs. Both of them do not correspond with the productivity of capital employed. Additionally, funds whether they are in the shape of equity or debt are pooled together for investment or day-to-day operations and are prone to same level of risk in the business. Since both are taking same level of risk, the question arises that why the providers of both be rewarded differently, i.e., one with interest and the other with gain or loss?

Talking purely from finance perspective, interest rate is one of the foundational variables in finance; all the financial models are structured on its basis. In general phenomenon of the interaction of market forces, the price of an item (in our case money) is decided ex-post. For instance, price of oranges is established after they are supplied in the market but when it comes to price for money, i.e., interest rates, they are defined ex-ante. They are established beforehand, and then, they are used in different models which are followed by real market activities in the form of supply and demand of financial assets. This makes it a tool to control the time value of money and not to price money.

To conclude, interest with its indigenous flaws has contributed more inefficiencies than its superficial benefits. It has proved detrimental to overall well-being of the society. Among many, widening societal gap is the prominent adversity it has inherited to the economies. The income disproportionalities and capital inefficiencies are amplified with the increased contribution of interest in economies. To alleviate financial distress, poor rely on borrowings, which have ultimately driven the concentration of wealth skewed toward the rich, hence rendering the poor even more financially crippled. The time has gone when interest can be fancied as a bridge between savers and borrowers to boost capital efficiency. Currently, the notion of justice is mercilessly defied when the toiled money of the small savers is being utilized by giant business industrialists, rewarding them back with as minimum as possible and piling the rest into their and banks' pockets, snowballing the disproportional wealth distribution. Conventional banks, deemed integral to the economy to the extent that often titled as "backbone of the economy," often play their part negligently, as they pass on the burden of increased interest rates to the borrowers, while depositors are left unrewarded for that surge. Conversely, when the interest rates are lowered, that does not relieve the borrowers from their financial cost. On the whole, banks use interest as a tool to exploit the interest rate movement giving least value to the society. Hence, the fabricated benefits of interest are no more a hidden story to even those who surfaced their intellectual economic theories on it. Artificial money creation, cascading inherent risk, and injustice are the outcomes of interest economies have experienced so far. Hence, Islamic prevention of interest is lucid and logical to safeguard the economy from such injuries.

Rent Related Issues

The worth probing issue, pertaining to land as a factor of production, is dealing with agriculture land. Unlike the industrial land, agriculture land has its unique property of fertility, which can be used by the ones who have the expertise; otherwise, the agriculture land resource would not be justifiably and efficiently used. But in some cases, the one who owns this resource is often incapable or uninterested to cultivate the land, so leaving him the option to lend the land to the party who can use it in resourceful manner. The issue arises when the compensation has to be given to the owner. As the ownership rights are still with the owner, but the effort and resources are participated by the agriculturalist, the profit of the crop has to justifiably portion to both parties. The compensation, according to some scholars, can be taken as cash, and according to others is share in crops, while some regard both of the forms.

The crop output cannot be ascertained at the time of contract, and imposing a flat preset amount would be the same as "riba." Hence, the landowner would be playing the same role to that of a bank, regardless of the crop end product; the landowner stays unconcerned to take his predefined share. A fixed quantity would be inequitable for both of the parties, depending upon the consequences. This can simply be evaded to preset the "proportion" of crop output rather than fixing the amount.

Islamic economic principles do not allow the preset owner's compensation as it can lead to injustice, hence favor the derived amount instead.

Let us consider two scenarios, i.e., (1) the owner of the land presets a flat amount before the crop has yielded any output let us say $20,000; (2) the owner agrees to take 40% of the share in the profits from the crop output. In first case, it would be unfair with both the parties as it is impossible to ascertain the exact crop output, especially when there are chances of the occurrence of natural calamities exist. The second scenario is fairer to both the parties as it is ex-post, i.e., based on the actual yield of crops.

Labor-Related Issues

Many remarkable theories of economics have extensively discussed the topic of labor, yet very few highlighted the question of compensating the labor justly. Labor though considered equally vital as other factors of production in Smith, Ricardo, Marx, and others' theories is often neglected in terms of how reasonably it should be remunerated. Islam emphasizes on pegging the wages of labor to the contribution it adds to the output. This logically avoids any injustice at both ends: labor and entrepreneur.

Issues arise when labor has to be remunerated before the output is finally processed. Had the wages be variable to the output of the production, the issues would be simpler, but pragmatically it is not that trivial to implement smoothly. It is quite impractical to peg the variable wage system altogether to output, especially when the business incurs losses. Moreover, the floor rate of wages also imposes another challenge to fix the wages to output.

Issues Related to Wages

Labor law entails the minimum floor to wages, below which recruiting labor is unlawful. Economic course books have generally disregarded the notion of flooring the wages, as it can lead to unemployment in the economy, hence detrimental for labor force. Though theoretically comprehensible, the minimum wage law cannot be ignored practically, as protecting labor rights has precedence over hypothetically assumed economic models. Islamic persistence on human rights of basic provisions can be one of the forms. The indefinite output dilemma can be simplified by sharing the profit. Profit can be a yardstick for pegged wages rather than market trend, to demonstrate more equitable treatment.

Conclusion

To conclude, in order to construct a well-integrated theory of profit, profit shall be as defined revenue minus cost. Second, the focal point of the theory shall be a firm instead of an entrepreneur. Additionally, it should be considered as the function of dynamic changes in business environment. Lastly, the profit may be shared between labor and capital in order to endorse fairness, growth, and peace in society. This type of profit theory will be acceptable in both conventional and Islamic trading frameworks.

References

Hasan, Z. (1975). *Theory of profit.* New Delhi: Vikas Publishing (Out of print).

Knight, F. H. (1921/1965). *Risk uncertainty and profit* (2nd ed.). New York: Houghton Muffin.

CHAPTER 5

Conventional and Islamic Trading Frameworks: Differences and Similarities

Abstract We discuss both the practical and philosophical similarities and differences between Islamic and conventional trading framework in this chapter. We discuss the permissibility principle in Islam which sets the basic premise of all types of dealings. We argue that Islamic trading framework includes whatever a conventional trading framework has except the forbidden parts. We discuss these forbidden parts in detail which include gharar, riba, risk shifting, etc. We also discuss the philosophical differences including property ownership, risk sharing and the impacts on economy. Islam seems to present a more comprehensive yet compatible trading framework to be practice, which not only suits Islamic world view but is also promoted to have positive impact on the economies at large.

Keywords Similarities · Differences · Islamic trading framework · Conventional trading framework

What Is Trading Framework?

Framework is a comprehensive arrangement of rules and regulations that administers and controls agreements, acts, decision making, etc. Trading is generally explained as the commercial exchange of goods and services. So, basically trading framework can be defined as a comprehensive

M. Ali and N. Zada, *The Islamic Finance Trading Framework*,
Palgrave CIBFR Studies in Islamic Finance,
https://doi.org/10.1007/978-3-319-96613-7_5

arrangement of rules and regulations that administers and controls agreements, acts, decision making related to commercial exchange of goods and services. In this chapter, our focus would be on describing the process of trading governed by Islamic principles (Shariah) as compared to as it has been governed under conventional legal system (common law).

Islamic trading framework is governed by Shariah law (Islamic law of contract), which has been discussed in detail in Chapter 2. Here, we will discuss differences and similarities between both the trading frameworks.

Differences and Similarities Between Conventional and Islamic Trading Frameworks

We will start introducing trade in Islam from a verse of Holy Quran, in which Allah SWT has compared between trade and interest and declares the permissibility of former and prohibition of latter.

الَّذِينَ يَأْكُلُونَ الرِّبَا لاَ يَقُومُونَ إِلاَّ كَمَا يَقُومُ الَّذِي يَتَخَبَّطُهُ الشَّيْطَانُ مِنَ الْمَسِّ ذَلِكَ بِأَنَّهُمْ قَالُوا إِنَّمَا الْبَيْعُ مِثْلُ الرِّبَا وَأَحَلَّ اللَّهُ الْبَيْعَ

وَحَرَّمَ الرِّبَا فَمَن جَاءهُ مَوْعِظَةٌ مِّن رَّبِّهِ فَانتَهَىَ فَلَهُ مَا سَلَفَ وَأَمْرُهُ إِلَى اللَّهِ وَمَنْ عَادَ فَأُوْلَئِكَ أَصْحَابُ النَّارِ هُمْ فِيهَا

خَالِدُون{2:275}

> *Those who devour usury will not stand except as stands one whom the Evil One by his touch Hath driven to madness. That is because they say: "Trade is like usury," but Allah hath permitted trade and forbidden usury. Those who after receiving direction from their Lord, desist, shall be pardoned for the past; their case is for Allah (to judge); but those who repeat (The offence) are Companions of the Fire; They will abide therein (for ever). (al-Baqarah 2:275)*

One of the most relevant words in this verse is Bai' which can be translated as an exchange of one object for another; one of the objects usually is the subject matter and the other being is considered as price. The Mejelle is considered as an authority on hanafi commercial law, describes a sale as "the exchange of property for property" with mutual consent. So in the broader context, Bai' can be used for any bilateral contract. So, we can simply translate it to exchange involving all sorts of trading activities. There are few exclusions from the set of exchanges; for instance, riba-based exchanges are universally prohibited. Likewise, exchanges that lead to complete uncertainties are not valid. As mentioned earlier, a trading activity in Islam must be free from all prohibited practices.

Different types of transactions (exchange) carry different bearings with respect to the liabilities and benefits for the involved parties. For instance, in a normal trading activity, one party passes on the property rights coupled with usufruct to the other party. In the case of Ijarah (as discussed in Chapters 2 and 3), which can also be called as the sale of usufruct, one party transfers usufruct for rental but holds the ownership, which eventually means that the later party would carry the ownership-related liabilities. Then, in contracts like loans, complete ownership along with usufruct of the underlying asset is transferred to the borrower for temporary time period. Borrower can use the asset and even generate income as he can do with his other belongings, but in this case after a stipulated time period the asset must go back to the lender. Another type of exchange is Musharakah, in which partners share the ownership, its benefits, and related liabilities as per the agreed terms and conditions.

In general trade transaction, ownership of the underlying asset is transferred as the sale agreement is agreed upon and signed by the parties. It is regardless of the payment terms which can be on cash or on credit basis. The most important thing in this regard is the consent of the parties. Unlike a loan transaction where the borrower after getting the temporary control on the underlying asset is supposed to return the same after agreed time, in deferred payment case, the buyer is responsible to pay the agreed price and not return the asset.

Now let us discuss how conventional trading framework or common law deals with these exchanges. Interest is one of the key factors in the loan and loan-related transactions. Contrary to Bai', which yields return on the basis of underlying risk, interest-based loan transactions contain the certain right of return. In Islam, "risk and reward" are vital elements of trade. Transactions/exchanges become usurious if they lack the elements of risk and reward.

Loan and trade (Bai'/exchange) are different and that constitutes the main difference between Islamic and conventional trading frameworks. A trade is said to be occurred when the underlying asset is completely in terms of ownership and once it is confirmed it becomes irreversible, which automatically means that the asset gets excluded from the ownership of the seller. As far as loans are concerned, ownership of the underlying asset is only passed on for a definite time period and same or similar asset is required to be paid back (Al-Jaziri, 1973). If the kinds of the goods to be traded are different from each other, one of items can be delivered on deferred basis. Example of this could be a credit sale or advance payment for ordering to manufacture a table through Istisna. In other words, if a currency is exchanged for edibles such as wheat, then it would not be considered as riba, but on the other hand if rice is exchanged for wheat on deferred basis, riba is found as they belong to same genus (Muslim, 1981, with annotation by Nawavi). Now let us talk about loan transactions, which are required to be fulfilled on equivalent basis for repayment purposes. Almost all the modern-day banking transactions fall under this imperative. The unequal exchanges in banking transaction show the presence of riba. That is why, since conventional banks buy and sell money, their trading cannot be called as Bai'.

Sarakhsi a renowned Hanafi jurist says: "Trade is of two kinds: permitted (Halal), which is called Bai' in the law; and prohibited (Haram), which is called Riba. Both are types of trade. Allah Almighty informs us, through the denial of the disbelievers, about the rational difference between exchange (Bai') and Riba, and says: 'That is because they said Bai' is like Riba'. Almighty, then, distinguishes between prohibition and permission by saying: 'And Allah has permitted sale and prohibited Riba'."

As in Al-Baqarah 2:275 (mentioned above), trade is considered as one of the commendable professions among countless legal ways of earnings. Islam as a way of life has recognized trade as a tremendous way of acquiring wealth.

Trading framework in Islam is based on divine knowledge source of which are Quran, Sunnah, Ijma, Qiyas, and Ijtihad. In the words of Addas (2008), "the Islamic trading framework is not a product of human thought resulting from any scientific inquiry: it is a ***divine direction*** leading to a ***unique*** way of earning legitimate profit." Trading framework in Islam is governed by Islamic law of commercial contracts.

Besides riba, there are a few supplementary issues which are diverging when it comes to Islamic law and conventional law (common or civil law). These issues are also important to be deliberated. These issues basically arise due to the differences in worldview. For instance, under Islamic law, the understanding is that all the properties are created and provided by God. This is clearly in contradiction with the modern secular mind-set as per which property is a secular item. This item may be redefined if needed. Another common way is to look for how legal system decides to value property claims. As far as Islamic law is concerned, property cannot be reduced, inviolable, and virtually supreme. Islam is minutely concerned with the way properties are acquired; that's why its lawfulness is discussed in detail in both the Quran and the Sunnah, which are considered above reason in Islamic jurisprudence. Islamic economic system promotes earning through fair and effective means. The primary things need to be considered are that other's rights should not have exploited. This way, economic activities would generate and whole society would get benefit. Islam emphasizes collective welfare over individual rights. Society at large takes preference in many instances. This concept is in line with modern thinking prevalent in the West, which tends to have started criticizing economic management through open-market approaches. The reason is that these approaches stress on economic growth without considering the impact on quality of life and increasing the income inequality in society. There is no doubt that Islamic religious principles are primarily in contrast to the principles of uncontrolled and ungoverned capitalism as they are viewed as posing threats to civilization by rejecting Shariah values.

The differences between Islamic and conventional trading framework have been summarized in Table 5.1.

The Philosophy of Risk-Sharing

Any discussion on profitability would not be considered complete without discussing the respective risks. Which brings us to another significant aspect of Islamic finance theory is that of risk-sharing. The conventional finance can be conceived as a game of spectators, where a big crowd watches a few skillful players playing in the ground. On the other hand, Islamic finance can be considered as a participatory sport, where everyone is involved and there is no spectator. Furthermore, there is perception of default moral blanket on all Islamic financial transactions. One of the most important aspects which are considered while making an investment is risk.

In ideal form of Islamic finance, the component of risk-sharing is supposed to be ingrained in the transactions. For instance, in the case of Mudarabah, those who provided finances for investment share risk of any loss in capital with the other part which carries out actual activities. The second party also bears the risk of losing their effort and time. On the other hand, in conventional finance, risk is left to be borne by specialists and is also traded among them. The risk is sometimes shifted and the

Table 5.1 Trading framework

Basis of difference	*Conventional trading framework*	*Islamic trading framework*
Religious belief	Secular and separates religion from other parts human life	Belief in unity of God and relates this belief to economic life of a man
Freedom of economic activity	In socialism, government enjoys economic freedom but in capitalism individuals enjoy freedom	Restrictive freedom is allowed in light of Shariah both by the government and/or individuals
Ownership of means	Socialism-state ownership Capitalism-individual ownership	Allah is the exclusive owner. Man is the caretaker of the property
Basis of economic system	Riba or interest	Interest free; PLS, zakat and compensation based
Competition	Socialism-no competition Capitalism-logical and unethical competition	Logical competition and financial cooperation
Wealth distribution	Socialism-equal Capitalism-unequal	Equitable

other times transferred to other parties. Mostly, the risk borne by parties is quite disproportionate as compared to the profits they make. For instance, banks provide investors with loans backed by collateral. That is how these financial institutions keep themselves covered from different kinds of risks like risks linked to marketing, production, and distribution, and their exposure is limited to the collateral related risk only. Islamic finance permits depositors who invest their monies with financial institutions to share the risks related to selecting the right type of investment and its respective success. On the other side, these financial institutions and banks advancing funds tend to share risks with the receivers of funds like manufacturers, farmers, traders, etc. Islamic finance lacks corporate governance which can allow depositors to have their say in investment decisions. There have been a number of alternatives proposed for this. And on the advances side, financial institutions can also be part of the decision-making process by becoming part of the board of directors of parties receiving the funds. The point to be noted here is that risk and respective responsibility for making decisions are (at least ideally supposed to be) spread across a greater number of concerned people.

Returns come with risk and for taking risk one needs to be responsible. So, if one party is sharing the risk, it is given right to have say in decision making. This helps for participation of a much greater segment of investors and entrepreneurs in economic activities, which makes them feel that they are one of the participants of the game rather than just spectators. And the benefits of involving wider range of participants are more than enhancing the feeling. It improves the bank stability. Indirectly, the surplus units (investment depositors) share risk with deficit units (firms) through the process of banking intermediation. By including deposits and investors under the umbrella of voters, Islamic banks can impact the profitability of the firms by influencing their corporate governance. To conclude, the banking sector's stability gets strengthened by the stability of the real sector. It results in the overall increase in integrity of the overall economic system.

Conclusion

This chapter discusses both the practical and philosophical similarities and differences between Islamic and conventional trading framework. A general rule of fiqh is worth mentioning here which is not only relevant to the trading but to all types of dealings; that is, the primary regulation governing all things in Islam is their permissibility. This means that everything is permissible except it is explicitly forbidden by Shariah law. Same is the case with trading frameworks; Islamic trading framework includes whatever a conventional trading framework has except the forbidden parts. We discuss these forbidden parts in detail which include gharar, riba, risk shifting, etc. We also discuss the philosophical differences including property ownership, risk-sharing, and the impacts on economy. Islam seems to present a more comprehensive yet compatible trading framework to be practiced, which not only suits Islamic world view but is also promoted to have positive impact on the economies at large.

References

Addas, W. A. J. (2008, January 15). *Methodology of economics: Secular versus Islamic* (MPRA).

Al-Jaziri, A. R. (1973). *Kitab al-fiqh ala mazahib al-arba'ah*. Mesir: Al-Maktabah at-Tijariyah.

CHAPTER 6

Issues Auxiliary to Islamic Trading Framework

Abstract This chapter explores issues auxiliary to Islamic trading framework. These issues include, government interventions, market structure, and business ethics. We argue that despite the failures markets have projected, their significance cannot be disregarded. The Islamic economic system entails markets based on strong ethical foundations where every individual's rights are sufficiently protected. Government's intervention is needed in dire issues, though not acceptable in form of artificially pampering the markets through tariffs, quota, etc. and creating dead weight loss, but surely in the events of income disproportionality, alarming poverty hikes, unfulfilled public needs, environmental degradation and the like. Although Islamic markets guidelines serves a platform of equity, honesty, justice and ethical system for common welfare, there is a need for a more focused approach for corporate social responsibility (CSR), an emergent notion in conventional economics.

Keywords Government interventions · Market structure · Business ethics

M. Ali and N. Zada, *The Islamic Finance Trading Framework*,
Palgrave CIBFR Studies in Islamic Finance,
https://doi.org/10.1007/978-3-319-96613-7_6

Introduction

The concept of market in today's world, with all its advancements and gadgets, has been evolved from a very primitive nature. Mainly, it was related to a common place for exchange of goods and services, commonly associated with open premises reserved for the merchants' stalls, and buyers gathering around them to buy the items they need. There was no compulsion of a permanent structured locality for the market place; rather, a first mover would have the right to secure his place in a lucrative site and others following him to make a structure of a market. This rudimentary concept of market has not vanished in today's innovative era; it still can be found in rural or underdeveloped areas of the world.

With this structure of unregulated and unsupervised nature, the market evolved to be being administered and regulated by an authority. In the beginning, this authority is composed of dominant people of the society making up committees to develop the rules of the game and oversee them. With the nascent needs, the committees standardized weights and measures and their practical usage. Subsequently came the need for developing the marketplace in a more orderly and convenient place. Therefore, other municipal facilities were added to the market place to make it a more comfortable place for trading. With the wave of rapid development in education, technology, infrastructure, and all facets of society, this evolution of market also underwent a drastic change in terms of facilities, structures, volume of goods and services, and most importantly the legal structure.

Presently, the word "market" is not even constrained to place or locality; rather, it may connote an altogether virtual marketplace, with buyers and sellers in different continents trading in fractions of minutes, harmonizing the prices throughout the marketplace due to information efficiency and legal proliferation. With incessant development, the transfers of ownership rights and legal frameworks have been continuously enacted by human interaction. The development in technology and automation, transaction efficiency, and infrastructure development have made the trade much more efficient and universal. It is not just the markets of gold and silver, which were harmonized and traded all over the world, markets of every kind of goods and services have been advanced to an extent that the most perishable items are also being transported to the other corner of the world with the least amount of time and resources. From the trade of giant items, like ships and airplanes, to the intangible services of research and innovation, the markets have turn out to be much more across the board.

With the radical development of present markets, we can still bifurcate these markets into two broad categories of those which include real goods and services, and those which aid in trade and settling, like financial tools, e.g., stocks, bills, certificates, bonds, etc.

Generally, Islam is being mistakenly alleged of disapproving advancement and development of present world order, whereas it is not the case in actuality. Islam does not only allow, but rather propagates the private ownership and trade proliferation. None of the Islamic laws place any hindrance in market rivalry or free operation of market forces. However, the market norms should not exploit any of the players in any terms. The market should promote societal well-being and a win-win game for all the players of the society. The market should follow the rules which are "Shari'ah compliant," and any defiance to the rules should promptly be addressed, as rooted back by the "Sunnah" of Prophet Muhammad (peace be upon him), when the unjustifiable practices of Jews were demonstrated in the pre-Islamic market rules.

Structure of Markets

Markets play the key role as the source of channelizing goods and services across the economy. This phenomenon makes the basis for valuing goods and services, commonly termed as "price" in market terms. Prices valued through free intersection of demand and supply forces are deemed fundamental economic driver of any society. In a free market, the price signals are triggered from buyers to the sellers, rendering it to be more resourceful and regimented. This bottom to top price estimation tends to minimize the market costs with the efficient allocation of scarce resources. This leads to a most ideal market structure, where there are no abnormal profits or any drainage in the form of taxes, tariffs, quotas, and subsidies. These kinds of market discrepancies due to artificial interventions create a deadweight loss in the form of misappropriations and disvalued scarce resources of the society, which may not be the case in the absence of such restraints. A free market with demand and supply valuing the price would render the economy much more affluent and self-regulated than one with artificial intervention.

Above-mentioned economic situation is based upon the condition that the market is perfectly competitive; otherwise, the scenario may not be fruitful as pictured. Assuming that the market has perfect competition requires that the product is a homogenous product, such that consumer may switch from one supplier to another rendering the market perfectly competitive. Another assumption supposed is the number of players in the market. A perfectly competitive market entails large number of buyers and sellers that results no bargaining power at either end and renders the market fully competitive. Another prerequisite is about the factors of production that can instantaneously be portable between any of the substitutes. And lastly the market players have full information about the market. With such set of assumptions, a perfect competition seems to be an experimental utopia which can only be achieved in a laboratory-controlled environment. Even if achieved so, the firms could sell unbarred at market price, few of them readily attain the control of monopoly, and the market would turn out to be imperfect.

Profit maximization and increasing the shareholders' wealth are the supreme goals of every for-profit organization. The spread between the input cost and the selling price of the end product is the vital part of the firms' earnings, accumulating to their shareholders' wealth. Had not the firms face rivalry of competitors, their innate profit-maximizing appetite would stimulate them to increase the prices unbarred. Hence, competition regulates the firms to earn normal profits. To ameliorate, firms try to overpower each other by adopting differentiation strategies in order to distinguish their product compared to their rivals. Branding, trademarking, marketing, and advertising are some of the strategies firms chose to setback their competitors. Apart from these, other strategies such as Cartels, embargos, quotas, tariffs, and taxes, created in order to bar the new entrants into the market, reduce the competition, and hence, markets may evolve to a monopoly in some cases. Henceforth, we experience the markets with the competition leftover by the firms inevitable for them. Issues with traditional market assumptions are discussed in the next section.

Issues with the Traditional Market Assumptions

The markets are constrained to exhibit perfect competition setup due to many inherited imperfections. Individual goals contradicting societal benefits result in market imperfections. With abundance of modern economics literature flooded with the advocacy of free markets, least we can find the shortcomings and failures these confront. Hence, referring here the most pertinent ones to the subject area is the need of the existing literature.

Markets in today's world, while serving the consumers, often disregard the basic pyramid of human needs. Usually, the upper tier of the hierarchy, pertaining to esteem and status, is addressed more than the basic physiological needs, i.e., food, shelter, water, etc. The higher margin opportunities for producing luxuries and status-oriented products instigate the markets to disproportionate the production of basic necessities of life. Serving the top niche market is more lucrative than producing bread and butter for a big chunk of society and hence shackles the underprivileged class. In a nutshell, the distorted resource allocation results in misappropriation of riches, widening the societal gap among the economies. Hence, there exists a need to probe this notion of modern consumerism.

Another dire issue of today's production processes pertains to rapid industrialization. The prices labeled on products comprised of the input costs paid by the producer. These input costs are only those which are materialized legally in contracts, and for which payment is made. There are many overlooked inputs, being used abundantly but are not paid for, used in production. These include natural utilities which are being under continuous contamination and depletion, but are still heartlessly exploited and taken for granted because they are not paid for. Had these natural resources be quantified and are added to the cost of production, the environmental scenario may improve. Any phenomenon that can add cost to the scarce resource used by producer may ameliorate the rapid environmental degradation present era is facing. However, a pragmatic framework of this kind has yet to be sorted.

Islam is often mistakenly regarded as a conservative system of religious beliefs shaping only spiritual lives of its followers, whereas it is a full code of conduct that influences every aspect of life one encounters. It not only focuses on individual nurturing, but also welfare of the whole society. In Islam, earning through business and trade is considered as the most esteemed and honorable means. Evidenced from the words of wisdom of great scholar and immediate follower of Prophet Muhammad (peace be upon him), Hazrat Ali who, while appointing governor of Egypt, wrote in the letter:

> …And all of these (soldiers, taxpayers, judges, administrators and secretaries) have no support but the merchants and the craftsmen through the

> goods which they bring together and the markets which they set up. These provide for the needs of (these) classes by acquiring with their own hand's goods to which the resources of do not attain… then make merchants and craftsmen your own concern and urge others to do so, for they are the basis of benefits and the means of attaining convenience. Tabatabai (1982, pp. 10, 14)

The supremacy of business in Islamic social setup can well be assessed through a fact that it has given the rank of "farz-e-kafaya." A "farz" is solemn responsibility of a Muslim, which is mandatory, whereas "farz-e-kafaya" is a responsibility of Muslims as members of society, which when performed by few of them, exempt others. Hence, joining business not only contributes positively to the economy by boosting the total output, it also serves as a vital means to earn God's reward. However, these rewards can only be materialized if undertaken with righteousness.

Due to innate voracity of wealth and riches, human being is always prone to overlook the morals and ethics of honesty, especially in businesses.

In Islam, consumer protection is the main focus of Islamic theology. Though extensively asserted by modern economic literature as well, consumer protection notion is a much different approach from implementation point of view. In Islam, morality is being inculcated in human personality, rather than surveillance and forceful imposition. In effect, if the virtue of honesty is not being nurtured by human souls, markets cannot exhibit successful upshots. The key features of Islamic market behavior can be summed up as follows.

First, Islam imposes a number of obligations on the sellers with regard to measurements, quality of goods, their prices, and provision of information to the buyer (Ghazali 1955, p. 75). It obligates Muslims to be extremely cautious while using weights and measures. As evidenced from numerous Quranic verses and Hadiths (sayings of Prophet Muhammad peace be upon him) pertaining to the subject area, honesty in trade is immensely apparent. "And give full measure whenever you measure, and weigh with the balance that is true: this will be (for your own) good, and best in the end (Quran 17:35)." The tradesmen should greatly concern about measuring and weights, and any smallest inevitable discrepancy should always be borne by themselves rather than consumers. "Give full measure, and be not among those who (unjustly) cause loss (to others by fraud) (Quran 26:181)." Apart from weight and measure, the quality of the produce should also meet the stipulated features.

Second, Islam also severely forbids overpricing by any artificial means like hoarding, blocking input materials, or any other means of creating scarceness. Some scholars advocate that margins should be capped and regulated, while others consider it to be the traders' own choice seemingly because forcing coercively is not as beneficial as self-instilled empathy.

Third, another distinctive feature of Islam in market s is abstaining merchants from unjustified praise of their goods. As narrated by Abu Hurrairah Prophet Muhammad said: "The taking of oaths makes the commodities sell, but it obliterates the blessing (therein)" (Bukhari 34:26). A market where hundreds and thousands of dollars are spent for marketing of products featured as the best and supreme one; Islam insists on disclosing even the minutest of defect of the product before selling it to buyer. This urges the producers to be meticulously careful about the quality of the product along the whole production chain. Right from buying inputs from suppliers, to the last phase of logistics and distribution, quality shouldn't be compromised at any cost, as any oblivious loss due to smallest defect or shortcoming does not exempt the seller from his responsibility.

This also normalizes the dazzling marketing contest today's markets are following in publicizing their products, exploiting consumer preferences, and wasting resources in least efficient means. Islam allows sales endeavors but in a realistic, humble, and productive manner.

Government Intervention and Islamic Trading Framework

Markets downturn and severe economic recessions have instigated researchers and policy-makers to conscientiously discover the reasons and remedies for such circumstances. The modern economic philosophies, as based on unrealistic assumptions, turned out to be futile in explaining such failures. Many economic policies were formulated in light of these works undertaken by researchers and policy-makers, aiming to sort out the causes and management of such economic failures, turned out to be unsuccessful in terms of efficient allocation of resources. Rather, some of the government policies aiming to control the circumstances by artificially adjusting the markets by tariffs, quotas, etc., worsened the economic condition with deadweight loss. From Islamic perspective, government plays an altogether distinctively different role from conventional ones discussed above.

Islam does not support the notion of restricted markets with artificial tools; in contrast, it propagates unbridled operations of the markets without defying Shari'ah rules. Any price hike due to scarcity of goods or increased demand should not be manipulated artificially and be treated inevitably. Role of government in an Islamic market is to stably plan, manage, produce and consume, and let the market's demand and supply intersect freely, rather than intervening and regulating intermittently.

Islamic concept of markets is refuted by some economists as inappropriate for the renowned notion of invisible hand of Adam Smith, i.e., unintended social benefits of an individual's self-interested actions—the phrase employed by Smith with respect to income distribution. As per Hassan (2008), this complete renounce is ill-considered. Self-interest is an innate weakness of human beings, and at times, setting it all free can lead to unfavorable circumstances. Therefore, free markets, though much required in Islamic system, are not indispensable to the extent that can lead to income inequalities and social disparities. Markets serve with respect to incomes; since the higher income segment tends to be more lucrative, it is served more with greater profit margins that leads to unmet needs of lower income group. Hence, Islamic system allows the government to ameliorate such deprivation of basic needs of people by channelizing, maneuvering, and directing the goods through appropriate strategies.

Islamic system of economics is based on the law (Shariah) created by the evidences from epochs of early Islam. Since monopolies never existed in those times, so does the renounce of them. However, as far as the public welfare is not endangered, there does not seem to be a cogent reason to refute them just because of their size. Rather, economies of scale and a bigger risk appetite may support their existence if the market demands are completely and efficiently met.

Business Ethics in Islam

Every religion in the world propels its followers to inculcate morality, integrity, uprightness, and truthfulness in their lives. Islam as a religion is not just a set of preaching and prayers pertain to individuals' private relationship with Almighty God; it is the religion encompassing full code of conduct of human's individual, social, economic, and political setup in holistic terms. This all-inclusive guide was projected at its best pragmatically by Prophet Muhammad (peace be upon him) as his own life, whom was entitled as "truthful" and "honest" even by his stanch opponents, and whose credibility was never challenged. Therefore, Islamic system profoundly emphasizes morality in every walk of life, particularly in trade dealings. Any act of fraud, deceit, and treachery is admonishingly condemned, as Prophet Muhammad (peace be upon him) said: "He who cheats is not of us, deceitfulness and fraud are the things that lead one to hell." A pertinent ayah in Quran pertaining to fairness and ethics is: "do not devour one another's property wrongfully, nor throw it before the judges in order to devour a portion of other's property sinfully and knowingly" (Quran 2:188). Moreover, another chapter of Quran stressing on honesty in trade dealings, among other numerous ones, says: "Woe unto those who give short measure. Those who, when they have to receive their due from (other) people, demand that it be given in full. But when they have to measure and weigh whatever they owe to others, give less than what is due"(Quran 83:1–3).

Picking evidences from Quran and Hadith, we can summarize the crux of Islamic market rules as follows:

Islam necessitates honesty and equity in businesses. It should be practiced holistically in every aspect of life inclusive of business and trade dealings. Pursuing lucrative opportunities to excel is not condemned; rather, toiling to earn within Islamic boundaries is considered "Ibadah" (religious noble deed). However, the lust of worldly riches should not intoxicate a Muslim to compromise his religious obligations of being honest, ethical, and just.

The competition in markets is considered healthy; however, an obsession to rule over the market rendering other players face a complete financial catastrophe is disregarded in Islam. Joining businesses is highly regarded in Islam, but with the role of positive contributor to the society.

In today's materialistic society, buyer and seller in order to increase their share of wealth may try to exploit each other's shortcomings. However, in Islam buyers and sellers are brothers to each other in first place, afterward comes the buyer–seller relationship. This builds kindness and goodwill among the market players, a very desirable trait in present markets. Accordingly, a buyer cannot exploit seller's weak position in terms of forceful transaction. Similarly, a seller should also abstain from misinforming, cheating, and deceit about the goods he is trading. Buyers and sellers can bargain while respecting each other's due rights.

Another key feature of Islamic market system is prohibition of certain kind of business (termed "haram" in Shariah). These include all forms of businesses that are detrimental to human's well-being both on individual and collective basis, such as wine, gambling, and pork.

Conclusion

Despite the failures markets have projected, their significance cannot be disregarded. The welfares they have contributed in the economies weighed sufficiently to absolve of their shortcomings. However, these downturns have directed us toward many valuable insights for taking preemptive actions in future. The Islamic economic system entails markets based on strong ethical foundations where every individual's rights are sufficiently protected. Government's intervention is needed in dire issues, though not acceptable in form of artificially pampering the markets through tariffs, quota, etc., and creating deadweight loss, but surely in the events of income disproportionality, alarming poverty hikes, unfulfilled public needs, environmental degradation, and the like. Although Islamic market guidelines serve a platform of equity, honesty, justice, and ethical system for common welfare, there is a need for a more focused approach for corporate social responsibility (CSR), an emergent notion in conventional economics. With rapid advancement and competition in the markets, an intensive methodology for instilling a socially responsible behavior among firms is looked-for in Islamic system.

References

Ghazali, A. H. (1955). *Ihya Ulum al-Din* (Urdu translation, Vol. 2). Lucknow: Raj Kumar Press.

Hasan, Z. (2008). *Theory of profit from Islamic perspective* (MPRA).

Tabatabai. (1982). *The spiritual life: Selections from Hazrat Ali's Nahj al-Balagha* (Translation with explanatory notes by W. C. Chittick, 2nd ed.). Tehran: Ansariyan Publications.

CHAPTER 7

Conclusion

Abstract This chapter provides a summary of the discussions in the book. We advocate that Islamic trading framework is an umbrella which shows the process of trading governed by Islamic Principles. It comprises the prohibitions, pricing, profitability, and other auxiliary issues like government intervention and ethical framework related to exchange of goods and services. Islamic trading framework appears to be more comprehensive yet compatible trading framework to be practiced in the contemporary world. Islam's framework is proved to be superior not only because of its moral values and compatibility with the modern philosophy but also because of its evidently positive impact on the economy and society at large.

Keywords Prohibitions · Pricing · Profitability · Auxiliary issues · Compatibility

From its nascent start in the last quarter of the previous century, Islamic finance has turned into an undeniable reality today. It is no more restricted to Muslim majority jurisdictions. Even the non-Muslim and secular jurisdictions have realized its importance and have initiated actions to develop Islamic finance in their respective jurisdictions; rather one can observe a race among different countries in becoming central hub for Islamic finance: "In 2014, the United Kingdom, Hong Kong,

M. Ali and N. Zada, *The Islamic Finance Trading Framework*,
Palgrave CIBFR Studies in Islamic Finance,
https://doi.org/10.1007/978-3-319-96613-7_7

and South Africa issued debut sovereign *ṣukūk* (or Islamic investment certificates), not so much to raise financing, but to make deeper inroads in the Islamic finance market" (Hayat & Malik, 2014, p. 11). Islam gives a lot of importance to trade and is considered as an alternative to interest Quran (2:275). This book has been written to present the structure of Islamic trading framework.

We have discussed the long standing issue of whether Islamic commercial law could give a comprehensive theory of contract or not. However, it is evident from the discussion in Chapter 2 of the book that Islamic commercial law has provided a comprehensive list of contracts that are permissible and those which are prohibited. Islam as a religion dis not abrogate the earlier practices, especially in the sphere of commerce and finance, out rightly. Instead, it cancelled only those contract which were based on exploitation and injustice. On the other hand, it retained some contracts in their entirety, as we shall see in the coming chapter, while modifications were introduced in a number of other contracts. We also observed that Islam has strictly prohibited riba in all its forms. However, Islamic law is unique in the sense that it also put a complete ban on gharar and this feature is not found in other religions. No wonder why Islamic finance was spared from the miseries of the global financial crisis in 2007–2008. Many practices and instrument especially those in the derivatives market could not find acceptance from Shariah scholars. Consequently Islamic financial institutions are by and large safe from such practices so far, with the exception of a few practices in some jurisdictions. Likewise, we also observed that consumer protection has a special space in Islamic commercial law and this is evident from the theory of options or khiyarat.

Chapter 3 elaborates on the nature, modes and types of contracts which are permissible under Islamic commercial law. We elucidate on some contested contracts found in contemporary Islamic finance sphere. In Chapter 3, an overview of the prominent Islamic commercial contracts and their application in Islamic finance was discussed. It is evident from the discussion that there are bunch of such contracts that are utilized to fulfil the needs of the customers in the Islamic finance industry. However, these contracts are not applied independently. Due to the complex nature of the products offered by financial institutions, these contracts are utilized in a group to design a particular product. This has been made possible due to financial engineering which is the backbone of the industry enabling to respond positively to the demands of the customers. However, there are certain risks involved in this financial engineering process because combination of contract in Shariah has certain parameters that need to be observed. Due to this, standard setting bodies especially AAOIFI has come up with detailed guidelines about the issue of combination of contracts and the different conditions that need to be observed in this connection. Overall, it can be seen that Islamic commercial has quite a number of contracts that can fulfil the demand of the contemporary complex business and finance arena. However, modification and adoption are at the core of this process and it is understandable due to the difference in time when Islamic law was developed and different circumstances that we have today.

Chapter 4 discusses the profit theory in mainstream economics, its issues and solutions provided by Islamic economics. The profit theory is an essential part of both Islamic and conventional trading frameworks. As discussed, in order to construct a well-integrated theory of profit, profit shall be defined revenue minus cost. Secondly, the focal point of the theory shall be a firm instead of an entrepreneur. Additionally, it should be considered as the function of dynamic changes in business environment. Lastly, the profit may be shared between labor and capital in order to endorse fairness, growth, and peace in society. This type of profit theory will be acceptable in both conventional and Islamic trading frameworks.

Chapter 5 discusses both the practical and philosophical similarities and differences between Islamic and conventional trading framework. This chapter is based on the general rule of fiqh i.e. the primary regulation governing all things in Islam is their permissibility. This means that everything is permissible except it is explicitly forbidden by shariah law. Same is the case with trading frameworks, Islamic trading framework includes whatever a conventional trading framework has except the forbidden parts. We discuss these forbidden parts in detail which include gharar, riba, risk shifting, etc. We also discuss the philosophical differences including property ownership, risk sharing and the impacts on economy. Islam seems to present a more comprehensive yet compatible trading framework to be practice, which not only suits Islamic world view but is also promoted to have positive impact on the economies at large.

The significance of markets cannot be disregarded. The welfares they have contributed in the economies weighed sufficiently to absolve of their shortcomings. However, these downturns have directed us towards many valuable insights for taking preemptive actions in future. The Islamic economic system entails markets based on strong ethical foundations where every individual's rights are sufficiently protected. These issued are termed as auxiliary which include the ethical dimension, government intervention, social and development goals. As discussed in Chapter 6, government's intervention is needed in dire issues, though not acceptable in form of artificially pampering the markets through tariffs, quota, etc. and creating dead weight loss, but surely in the events of income disproportionality, alarming poverty hikes, unfulfilled public needs, environmental degradation and the like. Although Islamic markets guidelines serves a platform of equity, honesty, justice and ethical system for common welfare, there is a need for a more focused approach for corporate social responsibility (CSR), an emergent notion in conventional economics. With rapid advancement and competition in the markets, an intensive methodology for instilling a social responsible behavior among firms is looked-for in Islamic system.

To conclude, Islamic trading framework is an umbrella which shows the process of trading governed by Islamic Principles. It comprises the prohibitions, pricing, profitability, and other auxiliary issues like government intervention and ethical framework related to exchange of goods and services. Islam's framework is proved to be superior not only because of its moral values and compatibility with the modern philosophy but also because of its evidently positive impact on the economy and society at large.

Reference

Hayat, U., & Malik, A. (2014, November). *Islamic finance: Ethics, concepts, practice*. CFA Institute Research Foundation L2014-3.

Index

M. Ali and N. Zada, *The Islamic Finance Trading Framework*,
Palgrave CIBFR Studies in Islamic Finance,
https://doi.org/10.1007/978-3-319-96613-7

S

T

U

V

W

Z

The manufacturer's authorised representative in the EU is Springer Nature Customer Service Centre GmbH, Europaplatz 3, 69115 Heidelberg, Germany. If you have any concerns regarding our products, please contact ProductSafety@springernature.com

Printed and bound by CPI Group (UK) Ltd, Croydon, CR0 4YY
30/09/2026
02225609-0001